EVERFLOWING LOVE:

ABIDING IN CHRIST

MARY IRWIN KILPATRICK

ISBN: 979-8-9863768-3-7

TABLE OF CONTENTS

FOREWORD

We have the privilege of walking and talking with God through His Spirit which indwells us. We were created for an intimate relationship with God. We were never meant to live and walk alone only in our own power. God loves us. He has done everything possible so that we can know Him.

As we abide in Him, He has the power to exchange our weakness for His strength, and to share His peace and wisdom with us. Only as we come to know Him and walk with Him daily, do we realize all that He wants to do in us and through us. Best of all we come to know His heart which is beautiful, loving and full of restorative grace.

I have spent many years learning to abide in the Lord, much of that time through intense trials. I can personally attest to His amazing love and faithfulness. He wants a personal, intimate relationship with us, and it is beautiful to walk with Him every day. I have experienced this in my own spiritual life and have witnessed many real and practical demonstrations of His love, power, and guidance. My life with Him provides fresh evidence of how He loves us, walks with us and provides for us. My sincere hope is that this book will help the one who is searching for Him to find Him and to trust in Him. Knowing Him and His love for you will change you. You will never be the same.

CHAPTER 1

ALIVE TO GOD

The Christian faith is unlike any other. It is founded not only on the basis of Christ's resurrection from the dead, but it teaches that each of us who believe in Christ as Savior and Lord have been born again into new life. God's Spirit has made us come alive spiritually, and we have been transferred from the kingdom of darkness into His kingdom of light. We have become alive unto God. We have new life within us that can now fellowship freely with the One who created us. We know that Christ has set us free from sin, because by His grace He paid the price for our sin.

As it says in Psalm 103:12, "As far as the east is from the west, so far has He removed our transgressions from us."

We are saved by grace. Yet many of us attempt to live the Christian life by our own efforts. We have not realized our birthright into the family of God. We don't understand what it is to be alive to God.

Romans 7:4 "Therefore, my brethren, you also were made to die to the Law through the body of Christ, so that you might be joined to another, to Him who was raised from the dead, in order that we might bear fruit for God."

And the life we live we live by faith, not by sight. For the love of God has been poured out through His Spirit which indwells us. We are alive to God as those who have been raised from the dead, holy and beloved.

Romans 6:11 "Even so consider yourselves to be dead to sin, but alive to God in Christ Jesus."

1

Many of us who are saved and born to new life in God receive instruction from other Christians that the Christian life is summed up in walking by the law. We get mired in Paul's dilemma in Romans 7:15-25, concurring that God's ways are the right ones, yet finding that we are practicing the very things which we know we shouldn't be. We lack the power in ourselves or our flesh to overcome the things which wage war against our souls. But Paul presses on and asks the question we have all felt at times, in our struggle with the flesh. Who will set us free?

Praise God that He inspired Paul to continue and give us the truth of Romans 8:1, "Therefore there is now no condemnation for those who are in Christ Jesus." We could have never been set free by the law, but God sent us a Savior who humbled Himself and was born as a man so that He might offer a sacrifice for sin once for all. By believing in Him, our spirits are born again into new life. We are quickened, we pass from death into life, and we are now able to walk by the Spirit as those who are alive to God. As Romans 8:6 says, "The mind set on the Spirit is life and peace."

As we read what Paul wrote it is obvious that we were never intended to dwell in Romans Chapter 7, with a roller coaster experience of trying hard to do what we know God wants, failing, feeling ashamed and trying harder the next time. We are incapable within ourselves and our efforts of ever attaining the freedom and the peace and the fellowship with God which we know should be our birthright as children of God.

So what does it mean to be alive to God, to be joined to Him? Romans 8:14 clearly states, "For all who are being led by the Spirit of God, these are sons of God." We have been adopted as sons and cry out, "Abba, Father." There is a tender heart relationship at the core of our spiritual union with God.

We are exhorted by older believers to read Scripture and grow in our faith, and so we should, for the words of Scripture are written for our benefit and often used by the Spirit to remind us of truth. As we read the words on the page it should make us hungry to know the One who inspired them and caused them to be written down for us. He is the One who sacrificed everything and who pursued a costly plan in order that we might know His heart and be able to join with Him becoming an intimate part of His family and His plan. The powerful God of the universe who spoke everything into existence just by His Word, is the One who wants above all else to have sweet communion with us. We were made for fellowship with Him, a beloved union of spirit to Spirit.

In the book of John when Jesus was talking with the Samaritan woman, He said that God must be worshipped in Spirit and in truth. When we believe in Jesus and His atoning work at the cross on our behalf, we believe that He was raised from the dead and was set free from the bonds of death so that our freedom could be purchased as well. It was a costly exchange, He suffered all and gave everything so that He could be our redeemer, pay the price for us, quicken us from the dead, make us spiritually alive and set us free.

A few years ago, during a sabbatical I spent with the Lord, He was teaching me more about His love and the immensity of what He offers to us. He spoke clearly through the Spirit and said, "Did you think that I came to the cross for such a small deliverance or tiny measure of love that you have been willing to settle for? A thousand times, NO!" His deliverance, His desire to set us completely free, to make us alive to God, encompasses so much more than we can hardly grasp. He does not offer us a little love, a little freedom, a small measure of spiritual life and unity with the Father. He lavishes us with grace, His love is everflowing towards us, the freedom He gives makes us soar with Him. He wants a tender heart relationship with us, where we can walk and talk together and cry out to our Father. When we are born again, our spirit comes alive, and we are indwelt with His Holy Spirit. We now have a heart connection and a Spirit that longs to be in total harmony and union with Him.

We read the words of Jesus in John. This was His last time with the disciples before the cross, and He wanted so much for them to understand. Yes, He was going away, but He would not leave them as orphans. In fact, it was to their advantage that He go away, so that the Holy Spirit would come. The Spirit of God would enable them to have the same type of relationship with God that Jesus had. Jesus repeated those words several times in John, chapters 14-17.

Jesus also talked about His disciples abiding with Him. The disciples would have understood the illustration of abiding in the vine clearly. The branches of the vineyard are pruned to bear fruit, they can do nothing by themselves. The life of the branches flows from the root source.

Ephesians 1:3 says, "Blessed be the God and Father of our Lord Jesus Christ, who has blessed us with every spiritual blessing in the heavenly places in Christ."

Our spiritual blessings are possible through Christ in our spiritual union with God. We settle for so little. I find that I have often clothed my Christian life with pitiful rags of self-effort trying to do things for God, instead of

4

spending time walking <u>with Him</u> and talking with Him. I cannot change a heart; I cannot know the deep need of someone else's heart. It is only when I spend time with God that He gives me insight into what He is doing and what He wants me to be doing. Jesus sought His Father continually for direction. He said this many times in Scripture, it was recorded in one instance in John 5.

John 5:19 says, "Therefore Jesus answered and was saying to them, 'Truly, truly, I say to you, the Son can do nothing of Himself, unless it is something He sees the Father doing; for whatever the Father does, these things the Son also does in like manner.'"

How do we know what the Father is doing unless we spend time talking about it with Him, and asking Him for direction? It shouldn't amaze me, but it still does every time, that when I spend time with my Lord, and He directs me to go to someone with a very specific message, it is exactly what they needed to hear at exactly the right time.

Oh, dear believer, the Holy Spirit within you longs to unite you to Christ and the Father in a tender walk which is personal, intimate, and beautiful. Even in the darkest of struggles, like those I experienced in my life for many years, He never forsakes us. He is beautifully there, reassuring us of His promises, speaking of His faithfulness, loving us. If we will draw near to Him, with open and yielded hearts, bringing everything to Him, trusting Him completely, He responds in ways that are patient, gracious, liberating, and loving. The more we hunger and thirst after Him and seek Him, the more we find that He has been pursuing us all along.

Why does the God of the universe seek to walk with us, who are sinful and weak and can offer Him so little? It was His desire and plan from the start. He originally put a spirit within man so that we could have fellowship with Him, and when that fellowship was broken, He has worked to restore it ever since. The only adequate answer is that He chooses to love us, overwhelmingly, amazingly. He lavishes us with grace. He is patient and teaches us as much as we are able to understand. We are so limited and often myopic, so slow to learn that if we will surrender everything into His care, we receive from Him the riches of what He intends for us. He brings treasures so much greater than what we could have ever imagined.

I am writing this book because He has told me it is time to do so. I have been mentored by other believers, many who were writers of the faith from previous generations, who made it their life's purpose to seek after God. My parents were missionaries, and my Dad was a pastor for many years. I learned many truths about God and His Word from an early age. My parents were people of faith who believed God and trusted Him. Yet there was little instruction when I sought to understand how to draw near to God.

In my early adult years, I made the mistake of attending a "Bible study" which was full of error, and which distorted the truth, elevating the leader of the group and his opinion rather than worshipping God in truth. This cult group led many young people astray, since the group spent considerable time reinterpreting the Scriptures, denying the deity of Christ, and elevating their own activities rather than seeking God. They spent time tearing down every other group of believers, and when I left this group, I found myself adrift. I was confused, and I wanted to know the truth of God's Word and more about Him.

The Lord pursued me and when I turned to Him, He gave me the sole desire to seek Him. I wanted to know the

God who had written the words in the Bible, who had given everything for me so that I could be saved. I asked Him for one thing only, that I could know Him. No doubt the Holy Spirit is the One who put that desire into my heart in the first place, but we always have a choice about which of our desires we will invest in and pursue.

It has been many years since I started on that journey, and God has taught me so many things and become my constant companion, my Sovereign Lord, my redeemer, creator, sustainer, and provider. He has given me songs in the night. He has caused all things to work together for good just as He promised in Romans 8:28, in spite of incredible difficulties. His Word has always been true. He has never left me or forsaken me; I have never been alone. It has been so beautiful to walk with Him. He has been completely faithful and walked with me and taught me through so many things. He has given me opportunities and blessings which have been astonishing, and which I never could have planned or foreseen.

Perhaps you too hunger to walk with Him, to know Him better, to trust Him more completely. This book is written so that it may offer some encouragement to you, a fellow traveler along life's journey who seeks after God. I love God's Word, and I love the Lord Himself, not for what He gives but for who He is. I sincerely pray that some of the things that He has taken the time to teach me might be of use to you in your journey.

If you love the Lord, you will know if these things are from Him, and you will search the Scriptures for yourself to see if they are so. If you seek Him, you will find Him, and it will be the most rewarding thing you will ever do. You will be changed; you will not be the same.

Blessed be the name of the Lord who ever leads us onward into beautiful and intimate union with Himself.

CHAPTER 2

HONESTY & HUMILITY

In any human relationship we only have true intimacy if we are honest and transparent with one another. Human beings often have hidden agendas, or we are afraid of exposing our "flaws" for fear that the other person will not like us, or worse, take advantage of what they know and use it against us. We are all sinful people, and we have been hurt by other sinful people. This can cause us to be wary of trusting, of opening ourselves up to total exposure. And sometimes we are hurt by our own perceptions of what someone else said, when in reality it might have just been our own anxiety or fear which caused the misunderstanding.

Communication is tricky between human beings, but oh so important. What was intended to be communicated can be unclear or misunderstood, not only from the one initiating it, but from the one receiving it. And yet true friendship and love is realized when someone knows us completely and accepts us for who we are and loves us anyway. When we find that type of relationship it produces a high degree of intimacy which is refreshing and affirming. We can be ourselves without fear. We can laugh together, have dialogue, be heard, share joys and sorrows, thoughts, and desires because trust has been built.

It is interesting that we sometimes apply our fears about people to our relationship with God. We are sometimes reluctant to be totally honest with God. I am amused when I find that tendency in myself, for He knows everything anyway! Nothing is hidden from Him. Yet when we are first learning to walk with Him, we tend to compartmentalize our lives and "allow" Him access to only parts of it.

Some people are ashamed of their past or their tendencies to pursue things which they believe are not pleasing to God. Most of us have spent years giving self and its desires free rein. We can often justify spending hours on our own pursuits because we have decided these are "good" activities. If we are truthful, we don't want to bring everything in our lives under the scrutiny of our conscience or talk them over with God because we want to retain control over what we want to do. We want to be our own boss. Wasn't that the issue in the beginning? Adam and Eve had a choice, to believe God or decide for themselves what they wanted to do. The choice has always been in our hands.

It is incredible to me the picture in Scripture of Revelation 3:20, "Behold, I stand at the door and knock; if anyone hears My voice and opens the door, I will come in to him and will dine with him, and he with Me." God is sovereign and has so much power that with just one spoken word He can create something out of nothing, or He can calm the wind or the sea. And yet He stands at the door and knocks and waits for us to open it. He wants intimacy with us, and it only happens if we are willing to open that door.

I was not always honest about the truth of my emotions or my actions, and I was helped in this area by reading the Psalms. The writers like King David were certainly not perfect, but I learned a lot from them about honesty before God. There is no real intimacy with God without being honest about everything in our lives and bringing it into the light of our relationship with Him. We sometimes think that if we do that we will be judged harshly, but I have found it is just the opposite. The Holy Spirit seeks to correct our thinking, expose the truth, and restore us to a loving relationship with our Father and Lord.

From my earliest years I longed to please people, which also meant that I developed to a high degree the ability to be motivated by guilt. Every morning for many years I woke up with a tape playing in my head of things from the day before or weeks before which I might have done better. I would feel guilty about it and work to try to change myself. I was locked into Romans 7 trying by self-effort to overcome my flaws and shortcomings. Since I am a sinful human being, there was plenty of material to work on!

I didn't really gain headway, in fact it produced over time the by-product of more anxiety, worry and guilt. I knew little of the freedom which the Scriptures talked about. I remained shackled to the rehashing of my sins, the worst of which was self-effort. Praise the Lord that Romans 8 was written, and useful for my benefit, and it starts with the words, "there is now no condemnation."

As we are transparent with the Lord and bring everything to Him, it opens the door for the Holy Spirit to address honestly the many things in our lives which need to be dealt with. He corrects our thinking and brings truth to our recollection, especially the truth of God's Word which is most applicable to our situation. He does not heap guilt or shame upon us. He wants us to confess, get clean, be set free, and wants to restore us quickly back to walking with Him right by His side.

I have known people who carried guilt and shame for many years. Subconsciously some of us feel that in this way we can atone for some of the things we have done, but it is not God's plan for us to waste years of our lives in this meaningless pursuit. He heals us spiritually, emotionally and sets us free to walk with Him in joy. All of that is possible when we give Him free access to every part of our lives, our thoughts, our memories, all of the things we dwell on or hang on to. The more honest we are, the greater is His capacity to liberate us, so that we can walk joyfully with Him into life in new ways.

In my early adult years, I experienced a relationship that was very abusive. I experienced physical and emotional pain which was devastating to me. Some years later, after I had begun to walk with the Lord in a deeper way, trusting Him and being open in every way I knew how, He asked me to take some time apart with Him. I have made it a habit of my life to have quiet times with the Lord, but at least once a year I take special sabbatical times apart to spend with Him. This was one of those special times. I had been reading a book about drawing close to the Lord, and it mentioned dealing with things from your past.

After I began praying, the Holy Spirit made it clear that I was still carrying pain from the past that I had not let go of. I knew it was important to be honest in every way with myself and the Lord. After I had settled myself in a quiet place, I took a sheet of paper and wrote down everything that caused me pain in my past, and in fact still caused me pain, every time I remembered it. There were more things on that list than I expected, including the pain of not belonging. I walked through the list with the Lord. I asked Him where He had been during those times in my life. He showed me that I had never turned to Him during any of those times. I was honest enough to acknowledge that was true. I had not invited Him into those situations with me.

We worked through the list together, and He healed me from all of the pain of the past in that one afternoon. Years of hurt were gone and did not return. I didn't know that was possible! He had waited for the right time, when I could face it honestly, and I was ready to walk through it with Him. I was able to entrust it to Him and let go of the pain. He showed me that these things had caused me to be fearful, especially about new relationships. After He set me free from the pain, He wanted to set me free from the fear as well. I then burned the list and started walking freely into what He had planned next.

We had moved three times in four years, and we had just settled in a new city. I decided to immediately start attending a women's Bible study at our new church. When I got there, I was early. The person leading the study said that the greeter was not going to be able to show up. She asked if I would be willing to greet everyone who came in. I felt myself stiffen up, remembering my past fear about meeting new people, but the Spirit whispered that I did not need to be afraid any longer. I relaxed and was able to greet everyone and started getting to know these wonderful women. It was only a few weeks later that they needed a substitute leader in Vacation Bible School, at the last minute, and they asked me. That launched me into children's ministry in the church and enabled me to be involved for years afterward in ministry to children and to women. All of that was possible because the Lord issued an invitation for me to be honest about my past, seek His healing and liberation, and then He restored me and set me free to walk without fear.

We cannot understand the preciousness of our Savior and our God unless we honestly embrace humility. We are so often full of self-justification, striving to make of ourselves more than we truly are. It becomes like a hamster wheel of continuous effort which never truly satisfies. Sometimes we compare ourselves to others, which either puffs us up or discourages us, neither of which is an accurate picture of who we are. Our attempts at self-worth are often based on a distorted identity. We have something of much more value. We have God-worth, which is not changeable. It does not depend on us, or how we feel, or on our appearance or who or what we compare ourselves to. He gave everything for us, He calls us His beloved. Colossians 3:12 says that we "have been chosen of God, holy and beloved."

He sacrificed His own beloved Son in order to save us, redeem us, and bring us close to Himself. He gives us life and light, and He abides with us. In humility we read the Scriptures and remember who He is. If I catch myself thinking too highly of myself or trying to give myself credit for what He has done, I go back and read Job 40, Isaiah 40 or other Scriptures which serve to remind me of who my God is.

Romans 11:33-36 tells us, "Oh, the depth of the riches both of the wisdom and knowledge of God! How unsearchable are His judgments and unfathomable His ways! For who has known the mind of the Lord, or who became His counselor? Or who has first given to Him that it might be paid back to him again? For from Him and through Him and to Him are all things. To Him be the glory forever. Amen."

This is the God who created and spoke into existence thousands of intricate life forms with an amazing variety of shapes, textures, purposes and patterns and the ability to reproduce after their kind. He created light and beautiful colors and sounds. We have so little understanding of even how the human body works together. I worked in a world class research university for a number of years. I sat in on high level meetings and a number of workshops where medical researchers were trying to understand and harness the power of one antigen which could bind to other cells in the body and be used to diagnose and then deliver therapeutic treatment to cancer patients. Researchers spend years on discovering the potential of just one little part of the human body. Yet it is our God who spoke it all into existence in the first place, with all of the body parts being able to harmoniously work together.

When we contemplate the power of our God and His amazing mind which we can barely comprehend, who are we that He should think of us? But it was His plan to not only think and care about us but to provide a way back for us, so that we could become alive to Him, to be one with Him, to walk closely heart to heart. He brings us understanding through His Holy Spirit so that even the smallest of His children can understand that He loves them, that Jesus died to save them.

One of the most important lessons I have learned is tied to honesty and humility. I walked through many years of intense trials, first through my own 4-year journey of pain and suffering and then for 25 years living in the valley of the shadow of death with my husband, John, who was told he could die at any moment due to his condition which was producing bleeding in his brain stem. They were years of pain and weakness, with instability physically and mentally and increasing limitations. During the last 8 years my husband endured the more extreme limitations of being a stroke victim who lost the use of one side of his body. One of the most important lessons we learned was that we do not have enough of anything. As much as I loved my family, I did not have enough love to give during every day of this journey. I grew weary and fatigued. I didn't always have enough patience, kindness, and strength. God had plenty, and He was more than willing to share what He had with me.

In humility as I face honestly my own weaknesses, and I bring them to the Lord, He exchanges my weakness for His strength. He taught me that I can admit my weakness to Him, my limited capacity to love, and then He taught me about His everflowing love. He showed me how to love others expecting nothing in return, because love is not given based on what is deserved. We simply have a choice to love freely and generously like He does.

When we acknowledge our weakness, the Lord encourages us. One day in March of 2000, John's heart started racing well over 200 beats a minute and it was out of rhythm. At the ER they quickly diagnosed him with atrial fibrillation (a-fib) and transferred him to the ICU. This was a tricky situation because although a-fib poses a significant risk of stroke, they couldn't give him blood thinners because he could bleed out in the brain. They needed to slow down his heart and convert it back to normal rhythm. They planned to do that by administering a chemical by IV. They started charging the paddles of the defibrillator. They explained that using a bag of these chemicals could make his heart stop, and they might have to resuscitate him. Even though I had worked in a hospital and even resuscitated people, this did not reassure me. I knew all too well the things that could go wrong. They needed to wait for the Doctor to arrive, and since I had a few minutes, I slipped out to the ICU waiting room for a moment to pray. It was very busy and noisy, so I quickly slipped into the bathroom. I rested my head against the wall and lifting my heart and my husband to the Lord I said, "Lord, I know you are faithful, but I wouldn't mind a little encouragement about now." Seconds later I opened the door and there stood a lady from my church right in front of me. She was as surprised as I was. She greeted me and told me the Lord had put me on her heart all day. The urge had become so strong that afternoon, she had to try to find me, and calling our house she had been told we were at the hospital. She had been searching for us all over the hospital. She literally said that the Lord had sent her to encourage us. A few seconds earlier or later and she and I would have missed each other. I gave her a big smile and a hug, and my heart began to sing. Yes, John still needed medical care, but the Lord was in control. The Lord of the universe who holds thousands of stars in the palm of his hand, had taken the time to bend down to whisper encouragement to one of his littlest children, and I knew I could trust Him to take care of my husband also. I returned to the ICU. They ended up using 2 bags of chemicals, and they were surprised that his heart did not stop. It resumed its normal rhythm. After a time of observation, we were able to go home.

When I acknowledge and bring my fear to Him, the Lord asks me to walk with Him, and He reminds me of His promises and His faithfulness. I am never alone. Time after time He has been faithful. At one point I was concerned because the physical and emotional care for my husband was taking a toll on me, and I didn't know if I would be able to have the strength to do this day after day and year after year. The Lord reminded me that His mercies are new every morning. As I walked with Him through each day, He gave me a fresh supply every morning.

All of these things made it clear to me that one of the keys to living in union with the Lord was to abide in Him continually. To do that I needed to continually be honest about my need of Him. In our current era of living in a fallen world, there is a lot of raw material for the Lord to work with so that we realize our need. In our culture we seem to think that being independent and self-sufficient are the end goals. If we are honest, we tend to think that acknowledging our helplessness is weakness and somehow makes us deficient. Praise God that it does!

We come to the Lord when we realize our need, first our need of a Savior and then usually later our need of Him in the midst of trials. It is often in the greatest trials where we see our greatest need and come in prayer, because we know we need Someone outside of ourselves to intervene. But what if we were honest enough to see our need every day? What if we acknowledged that we are never enough on our own, and that what we have to offer is pitiful compared to the amazing storehouses of grace which the Lord can provide if we only abide in Him?

The beauty of being left in trials for a long while is that after you have seen Him meet your need time after time, you start seeking Him not for the fulfillment of a need, but simply because it is beautiful to walk with Him. You no longer have any desire to live without Him. He brings such joy to your soul; His presence makes you so glad that you want to share everything with Him. He is light and life and His purposes are eternal. Why would I want to exchange that for temporary and petty desires that never satisfy?

He becomes our delight. He is the lover of our soul. We are his bride, and He is the bridegroom. My desire grows to plan special times together with Him, to talk about everything, to trust Him with everything. I love to walk through creation with the God who created it, expressing my pleasure at what He has done and who He is. As we abide in Him, He abides with us. It is an exciting thought that His desire is to spend time with us, that He delights in us. Jude 1:1 says that we "are the called, beloved in God the Father, and kept for Jesus Christ."

There is so much His Spirit wants to teach us. There is so much we need to understand and grow into. But He is patient with the growing process, for He is not developing with us a relationship for only a season, but for eternity. He often waits until I can understand His truth more thoroughly, His timing is always very precise. Then He teaches me things in very vivid ways which I can never forget. His truths are everlasting. Thanks be to my God, for my growth and my walk with Him do not depend on me. Philippians 1:6 says that He was the one who began a good work in us, and He will carry it out until completion. He works with great power to help His children who believe. Ephesians 1:18-19 is a prayer that our "hearts may be enlightened", that we will "know what is the hope of His calling" and know "the surpassing greatness of His power toward us who believe."

Dear believer, are you willing to honestly and humbly give up your dearly held opinions and self-justifications and your desire "to be right" so that you may gain Christ? Are you willing to lay aside your desires for earthly things that you may follow and know Christ? The adventure with Him is beyond compare. The truth He brings is transformative, enlarging the soul and the mind and making it possible to truly be alive to God even in the midst of a fallen world. Do you truly want to know the love of God which not only enraptures your own soul, but equips you to love others? Start with honesty and humility before God in everything.

Let me add one word about confession that I have learned. Many sincere Christians spend much time in confession. As the Lord reveals our sin to us and we maintain humility before Him, confession is important for our spiritual life. Scripture instructs us to confess our sins and that He will be faithful and just to forgive us our sins. 1 John 1:9 says, "If we confess our sins, He is faithful and righteous to forgive us our sins and to cleanse us from all unrighteousness." And the wonder of it is, as it says in Psalm 103:12, "As far as the east is from the west, so far has He removed our transgressions from us." However, endlessly reviewing the ways we have sinned is like picking up and hugging a garbage can. We sort through the pieces of garbage and at the end have a carefully catalogued pile of sin. This means we have spent much time just looking at ourselves. There are times that even in confession our self can intrude and make it all about us. It is much more instructive to spend our time gazing at the Lord, spending time talking with Him, and focusing on who He is and His purposes.

As we spend time honestly with the Holy Spirit, He is faithful to point out when we need to deal with sin. As we humbly keep short accounts with Him, we confess our sin when He shows it to us, and we know that our sin is forgiven. We can return quickly to His side in full fellowship. That way we can spend most of our time walking and talking with Him and fulfilling the purposes for which He calls us, paying attention to what He wants to do. Often He purposes to bring people into my life on which I need to be focused, rather than being focused on myself. As His light shines into my life, He will point out any darkness to be dealt with. I find my time better spent dwelling with Him in the light. We have a love relationship with Him. As we are honest and humble, we agree with Him about our sin. We don't want anything to come between us that would alter the intimate and loving relationship we have with Him.

We want to walk with Him closely, and anything that impairs that becomes grievous to us, just as it grieves the Holy Spirit. It is like having the closest of human relationships in a wonderful marriage, and the slightest disagreement or conflict is painful to us because it mars the beautiful harmony and unity we have with each other. That conflict can affect our intimacy. We learn in humility to come with an open heart and talk transparently about it. We don't have to spend time justifying our actions or why we are "right," but rather agree on the truth together and restore the harmony and oneness of purpose, mind and heart which are so precious. Jesus talked a lot in the upper room about unity, about believers loving each other. There can be no unity without humility and honesty.

Humility also allows us to open up to wonderful teachable moments as we study God's Word. God inspired the Scriptures to be written for our benefit. The Israelites were coming out of a pagan nation where they had lived for generations. They knew nothing about the sovereignty and holiness of the one true God who was leading them out of Egypt. They knew precious little about how a people should act toward one another. All of the commandments were put in place to guide and lead them. If they would obey them, it would protect their lives, their families, and their nation from harm. The common thread woven through all of the commandments was the love of God and how to act in love with each other.

As sinful human beings, people did what we all tend to do, see how far you can push the boundaries of the rules, or in many cases break them altogether when it is expedient. We have all at various times wanted to be our own god, make our own rules, create exceptions for ourselves in order to fulfill our desires or justify our actions. Jesus said in Matthew 15:8, "This people honors Me with their lips, but their heart is far away from Me."

The new covenant ushered in a heart life, a new Spirit which would dwell in those who are born of the Spirit, who become the children of God. Jesus astonished many people by calling God His Father, and He alienated many of the teachers of the law by claiming to be one with God. They were shocked at the blasphemy, but it was only blasphemous and shocking if it were untrue.

Some, like Nicodemus, came to find out the truth. He was confronted by a supremely teachable moment. John 3:9-10 gives us the details, "Nicodemus said to Him, 'How can these things be?' Jesus answered and said to him, 'Are you the teacher of Israel and do not understand these things?'" Would Nicodemus have the humility to accept that God's truth was very different from the opinions and carefully crafted beliefs that he had held onto for so long, and had in fact taught to others?

We all face the same thing as we draw near to God in Spirit and in truth. Will we allow Him to change us? Will we have the humility to be taught by Him? When He shows us truth or asks us to obey Him, what will our decision be? This is important even in little acts of obedience.

As I started abiding with Christ, the Holy Spirit asked me to obey Him in many little ways at first. I quickly realized that I liked to decide things for myself and wanted to justify myself when I didn't obey. I determined not to make excuses for my actions and to be honest about my lack of obedience.

One of the areas the Lord worked on with me was my habit of worrying. How could I say that I trusted God and yet I worried over so many things? Was I going to trust Him or not? I determined not to indulge in excuses for my worrying. Over time as I stopped myself and came to the Lord with worry, fear, and anxiety and put it all into His hands instead, my habit of worrying was gradually removed. I hadn't realized how weighed down with it I had become, how it permeated my thoughts and burdened me. I could not change the present or the future by worrying about it, and I burdened myself excessively by worrying about the past. How could I believe Matthew 11:28-29 about coming to Jesus and finding rest and yet get cozy with a life of worry? It is absolutely critical that we are honest and humble enough to acknowledge the truth when the Holy Spirit points it out.

The Lord has asked me to obey Him in many areas in a variety of ways. Even in the smallest things, if I disobey or ignore Him, it breaks the sweet fellowship we have until it is dealt with. And this is even more critical as we live a life of obedience in following the Lord's purposes in our lives and the lives of others. If the Lord points out a right or left turn that He wants us to make in our day, do we pay attention? Or are we so engrossed with our plans, our checklists for the day, our desires for what we want to accomplish that we miss altogether the heavenly appointment He wants to send our way?

There are so many people who need encouragement, a gracious word at the right time. How many times have I told someone I would pray for them rather than take the time to put my arm around them and pray with them right then? I had a dear brother in the Lord who taught me this so clearly. I was in the midst of a heavy time of my husband's suffering. I was able to arrange for his care and went to church briefly, but I needed to hurry home afterward. This brother spotted me, and even though he was busy and in a leadership position in the church with things going on that morning, he turned aside. He asked me how it was going, and I honestly explained what we were walking through. He immediately asked if he could pray with me right then. He placed his hand on my shoulder, and we went to the throne of grace together. He not only asked for the help I needed from the right source, but the love and care he displayed touched my heart deeply. He was a demonstration of God's love to me at just the right time. God intended for him to do that, and he clearly got it.

Are we willing to be God's feet and arms and blessing, in the midst of our busy days? God has given me messages at times to certain people. It is amazing the precision of the words and the timing. It has impacted their lives in surprising and loving ways, and it has impacted their hearts in ways I cannot even see. They have expressed this to me, but it was God who orchestrated all of it. I was only an obedient child delivering a message. And it has blessed me to be a part of it. God could have sent someone else, and perhaps in other situations when I didn't pay attention, He did use someone else. How blessed I have been when my little acts of obedience have blessed others, and He has shown me a little of what He is doing in their hearts and lives.

There is no real growth in the Christian life, no real abiding in Christ without our desire to love Him and obey

Him. He is after all, Lord of Lords, and King of Kings. The longer I have spent getting to know Him and love Him, the more my faith has grown in who He is and how utterly trustworthy He is. My first little attempts at believing Him and trusting Him have blossomed into a confidence in my loving heavenly Father and how completely He blesses us when we follow Him in obedience and with glad hearts.

We are His children, and we can come running with happy feet into His throne room ready to humbly and honestly talk about everything in our lives with Him. We get to seek His knowledge and wisdom and find help in our time of need. We can choose to lovingly carry out His will because we trust Him and His plans. We are confident in His goodness, and we know we are completely loved.

CHAPTER 3

SURRENDER

Many people ask questions about how to walk with God. I asked those same questions as a young believer and did not find much instruction or help for quite a while. I find that incredibly sad. We spend a lot of time talking about discipling young believers. We correctly teach them about studying their Bible and having prayer time, which are both essential. I have found precious little said about developing a heart relationship with Christ, not just for salvation, but for everyday life.

Often there seems to be a long time between young believers knowing they have a Savior, and the realization that He is Lord, not just positionally but practically every day. If we are honest, we think sometimes that if we acknowledge Him as Lord, He may "lord it over us." We look at verses such as Luke 9:23 which talks about denying self and taking up your cross as too costly, how could we possibly do that, especially day after day? The idea of lordship is foreign to us.

We rightfully conclude that human slavery throughout history has been an abominable act when someone is subjugating and demeaning another human being and making them less than they are. We know that every person has worth, has a right to human dignity and is of inestimable value. I grew up in third world countries with a goal to bring the love of God to everyone that we encountered because they were loved by Him and precious. In the context of our relationship with God, we at times bring some of this thinking about what being enslaved means, and we don't want to be subject to God's rule.

If we are completely honest with ourselves, we think the Lord is asking too much, and He will probably make us give up what we want most. Or perhaps we think if we give Him the place of Lordship and surrender our lives to Him, He will want us to move to the farthest reaches of the planet where we will hardly be able to eke out a life for ourselves, we will be out of our comfort zone and not have the blessings of home. We fear that we would be treated badly and be surrounded by a foreign language or strange culture.

What we fail to realize is that giving Him the place of Lord in our lives has always been voluntary. We are not subjugated, we are not forced, we are not made of lesser value. On the contrary, we find that we are beloved sons and daughters of the most High God. We are welcomed to His banquet table to feast in an atmosphere of love, acceptance, forgiveness, and grace.

The Lord whom we serve is wise, good, kind, gentle, patient, faithful, all powerful, full of grace and truth. If we hold onto our life and live it our way, do you have any idea what we will be missing? We will be left with only our own resources, our own "wisdom," our own limited supply and best efforts at pursuing our self-centered desires which bring us at the most momentary and very transient pleasure. And at the least, we end up with broken promises, disappointed relationships, and a short supply of anything of real value.

Not only does it hinder us not to be in proper relationship with Him, but it shortchanges the people around us. We could be abiding and connected to our Lord who gives all things in abundance. We could be living a life of faith and fellowship, full of grace and being used by God for eternal and meaningful purposes. We could have fullness of joy, even in the midst of incredible challenges. We could have His fellowship, His comfort, His unlimited supply of strength, peace, and wisdom. How little we are willing to settle for sometimes!!

Walking with God means that we do not just surrender our lives to Him in a one-time event, although that is certainly necessary and valuable. We must live a daily life of surrendering our hearts, minds, time, talents, everything into His keeping. It goes hand in hand with trusting Him. When I was younger in the faith, daunting challenges would make me go running to the Lord. I knew I needed to bring these things to Him in prayer and ask for His help and trust Him with it. I certainly couldn't handle it on my own.

It reminds me greatly of the Israelites who in the midst of their struggles, especially with neighboring countries and conquerors, would bring their great need to the Lord. The Lord would rescue them, but afterwards they would return to doing everything on their own. Similarly in times of great personal need, I would seek the Lord's help. He was gracious and met my need, although often in ways and in a timing I did not expect.

I remember vividly when the Holy Spirit helped me to ask the question, "What if I trusted the Lord for everything, every day?" It was a novel idea for some reason. You would think this would be a natural concept for a believer to embrace, but it was not common in the believers or churches where I attended. Being saved by grace was taught clearly and scripturally but living by grace daily in a love relationship with the God who saved us and who was our Lord, was not clearly communicated.

So, it was a watershed event in my Christian life to start trusting the Lord in everything.

I started living each day bringing everything into His presence and talking it over with Him. To be honest, during this time I was working a job five days a week, so I can't say that during my working hours I always brought every matter of my business day to Him. I improved in that area later, realizing just how much wisdom I lacked and how much I needed His wisdom every day! But I remember the profound impact in my spiritual life that happened when I started trusting Christ daily and walking with Him. As I opened my mind and heart in every area to Him, and honestly and humbly asked for His truth and guidance, I also surrendered to obeying Him. Often the Holy Spirit would bring Scripture I knew or was studying to enlighten me. But there were many instances of His applying truth and guidance specifically for the matter at hand.

Surrender is really the key to abiding in Him. A branch cannot stand off by itself, even though it acknowledges who God is, and at the same time still be connected to the vine. Abiding is essential and only possible when we are living the yielded life, remaining connected to the vine which is the author and source of its life and through which every good thing comes from our loving heavenly Father.

We were in the midst of our walk in the valley of the shadow, when it became clear that my husband's heart was starting to go out of rhythm every day and racing along at a dangerous speed. His brain condition made it impossible to take blood thinners to mitigate the danger, and he was at high risk for having a stroke. His heart specialist decided to do an experimental surgery of a special type of ablation to burn a maze in his heart which should help with the erratic and fast paced signals. They were also going to remove the left atrial appendage on his heart which is the part most prone to producing strokes. This special ablation procedure was new and had never been attempted in our part of the country, so it was attended by many experts and watched very closely.

Unfortunately, with his comorbidities, John was not exactly a prime candidate for a successful experiment. After the surgery, his oxygen plummeted, and he was put on a ventilator. When his lungs recovered sufficiently, he was moved to a private room. I had worked in ICU's before in my early career, and I was used to taking care of patients on ventilators. Even so, he had more tubes and monitors placed in and around him than I had ever seen. As he started resuming consciousness, his pain levels shot through the roof, despite the pain control medications they already had going. He was in such distress that his body was arching off the bed in agony. They ran for morphine shot after morphine shot, before he relaxed into a somewhat sedated rest.

They assured me he would be sleeping for a while, so I slipped downstairs into a garden on the hospital grounds. In prayer I poured out my distress at seeing the pain my husband was enduring. I cried out to the Lord. He responded by immersing me in His peace. I had heard and sung about "peace like a river." I was now in the midst of one. This peace was flowing into my mind and my spirit and there was no end to it. It had depths I could not understand or get to the bottom of. I was completely at rest, my heart sharing in the peace of God which was totally beyond my understanding. John stayed in the hospital for 30 days. That whole time we were both surrounded by God's peace and able to rest in it. There were some unintended complications of the surgery, which the doctors took note of and learned from. Ultimately the surgery was successful and did its work of keeping John's heart steady. It was during this time that I realized some fundamental truths.

The fruits of the Spirit only come as we stay connected to the vine, abiding in Him. When we are alive to Him, in union with Him, He can share who He is with us. The fruits of the Spirit are God's, and He is freely willing to share them with us. He is love, He is peace, He is faithful, He is wise. Like it says in Philippians 4:19, "And my God will supply all your needs according to His riches in glory in Christ Jesus." He knows what we lack and can help us, not as we stand afar off but as we stay connected, for then He can share Himself with us. It was an immensely valuable lesson. I had no idea that things were going to get harder. John would suffer a stroke in a few years, and I would need the mercies of God which He could supply every morning, moment by moment.

Do you hesitate to surrender everything into His keeping? Oh, if we only trusted Him like we should. He is not faithful sometimes, loving sometimes, wise sometimes. His character can always be trusted, His purposes are always of eternal value. He is the one who delights our souls. As the Word tells us in Philippians 3:7-8, anything we count as loss will be more than compensated by what we gain from knowing Him, which is so much more valuable. The most beautiful thing of all is that we will be connected to His heart, continually. We will be open to receiving His tender loving care and His strength, and we will find that His promises are all ours. He will get all of the glory, and we will gain knowing Him intimately.

To remain connected to the vine we must remain yielded and open with no barriers between us which would hinder the flow of living water. Do we want to provide living water to those around us and fulfill the purposes for which we are called?

On the West Coast many people have sprinkler systems built into their lawns. These remind me of God's truth about living water. I have often asked God to help me be an oasis where people can come, so that I can point the way to living water, pray with them, share God's truth with them, try to be His ambassador of grace. As Christians we are much like sprinkler heads which have the ability to give out water in our areas of influence. The water's source does not come from the sprinkler head; it flows through the pipes. In order for the water to flow, we must make sure the pipes between the sprinkler head and the source of water are kept clear and open. Just so the connection between us and the Lord must be kept open, so that we have truth and living water to share. It is flowing from Him into us. Our relationship with Him must be fresh and completely connected to have an adequate and abundant free flow of fresh living water.

Sprinkler heads are sometimes impaired from deploying because there is grass which grows over them, impeding them from functioning and dispensing the life-giving water. It is the same in our lives sometimes. We have grown so busy with our own work, our own plans and purposes, that we have let those things totally grow over and impair our ability or our readiness to share the things which really matter. We sometimes severely limit the time we have available to even care about being able to give water where it is most needed. We already have received and experienced the life-giving water which leads to eternal life, but what about those with whom we come into contact? How many are discouraged, without hope, feeling unloved, or just need encouragement for the day to walk more closely to their Lord? What have we allowed to grow which is getting in the way of loving others enough to truly see them and meet their needs in the loving way in which the Lord wants us to refresh them? Oh, that we would continue to stay completely connected to Him, loving Him, and realizing the importance of removing whatever holds us back from giving out His living water.

Surrender is not a word that our society values very highly, but it is vital to our union with God. Paul urged us in Romans 12:1-2 to present ourselves to God which would be our "spiritual service of worship" and to be "transformed by the renewing of your mind." If we do that, then we will know that the will of God is good and perfect. The cost of surrender is nothing compared to the cost of what you will give up by not knowing Him or not staying connected to Him. Surrendering to the God who made us, who loves us so completely, who is good and full of light and life, becomes the most blessed union imaginable, full of unspeakable joy and so much more.

CHAPTER 4

THE PRAYER OF RELINQUISHMENT

Closely related to surrendering and trusting everything in our lives to God is the prayer of relinquishment. I have heard many times from various sources that we should "claim the promises of God." I can certainly relate to "standing on the promises of God my Savior." Many are His wondrous promises and His provision for us. Especially in difficult times, His promises bring peace to my soul for I know that He is faithful and is a promise-keeping God. However, too often I have seen Christians find a promise in Scripture which they are determined to put into the context of what they need at the moment, rather than wait on God to fulfill their need in His timing and in His way. I have been tempted to do the same at times. It results in trying to hold the Lord hostage to a phrase from His Word without allowing for the sovereignty and wisdom of God to bring the fulfillment of His promises how and when He knows it is best. It short circuits trusting in His faithfulness to do what is good at the right time. It also robs us of walking in a beautiful heart relationship with Him, humbly keeping our heart centered on the One who walks with us step by step. He has so much to teach us along the way, and He longs to walk in a tender relationship with us.

It reminds me of Jesus in His temptation in the wilderness. He was surely hungry but responded to the tempter's words in the wilderness about making stones into bread by saying in Matthew 4:4, "It is written, man shall not live on bread alone, but on every word that

35

proceeds out of the mouth of God." Jesus was in close fellowship with God and followed His every direction. His words to the tempter could have meant that His bread was to only obey God, but I find it interesting that God the Father had not told Him to make the stones into bread, and so Jesus didn't. At the end of His temptations, God sent angels to minister to Jesus at the proper time. Likewise, in Gethsemane Jesus would have preferred to avoid the coming ordeal but had set Himself to do things the way the Father had planned, not according to His own wishes. Jesus lived the surrendered life.

Philippians 2:8 "Being found in appearance as a man, He humbled Himself by becoming obedient to the point of death, even death on a cross."

So how do we surrender everything into His care? The prayer of relinquishment is the powerful answer. It is powerful because it takes who we are and what we care about and puts those things into the hands of One who knows so much more than we do.

In the Scriptures we have a picture of the Lord who stands at the door and knocks. He has always waited for us to invite Him in, whether it is for salvation or daily walking with Him. It is easy for us to shut Him out, for us to run off on our own, ready to "fix things." The longer I live the more I understand how little I really have what it takes to accomplish much of value. But when the Lord starts working, amazing things happen. He is the only one who can change hearts. His timing is always perfect. When I try to do things, my timing and my methods may have some benefit to me, but they are often short sighted and inconsiderate of the needs of others around me. He sees the whole picture and is working in many lives at the same time.

I often think of the story of Hezekiah in the Bible. As king of Israel, 2 Kings 18 says that Hezekiah trusted in the Lord and clung to the Lord. At one point in his reign, he was beset by his enemies the Assyrians, who mocked the God of Israel and said they were going to overthrow Judah. In 2 Kings 19:14 it tells us that Hezekiah took their threatening letter and spread it before the Lord. It is a beautiful picture of humility on the king's part. He knew he needed the Lord to handle the situation in ways that he could not. I have often come to the Lord and spread my day or my particular problem out before Him. Rather than follow my checklist of things to do, He illuminates my mind to know what things to make a priority for the day, and what I need to let go of. There have been a number of times He has told me to rest or to come walk with Him during my lunch hour. When He first started telling me to rest, I marveled. I have a strong work ethic and felt that I couldn't take time to relax my mind during the day or turn away from my work for a few minutes. But I found that rather than hinder my work, it enhanced it. The brief time which I took for a walk with the Lord or rested from my work gave me more focus and energy. I gained an entirely new perspective on the problems I needed to address or the work I needed to do. Even more importantly, it gave me fresh eyes to see the people around me with a renewed focus on caring about what they needed. And the best part was that I got to walk in close fellowship with the Lord, which is always so amazingly refreshing and life changing.

The prayer of relinquishment is powerful when it comes to surrender. The most difficult thing we deal with on a daily basis is ourselves. We are often consumed with our needs, our limited perspective, our problems to be solved, our worries and anxieties over so many things. Daily, even moment by moment, we must learn to relinquish our lives into the hands of our Heavenly Father. The Holy Spirit who indwells believers is waiting for us to yield to His Lordship in our lives. He is so loving, kind and good. He encourages us and brings truth to our minds. He is the great comforter. He gives us an entirely new perspective. He keeps us in the abiding relationship so that all of our weaknesses and limitations are overcome by His sufficiency. He supplies so much of what we really need, starting with His love and grace. He gives us clarity on how to address things. If we let Him, He removes our fear and anxiety as we trust in Him.

We say that we are believers. What are we believing? We say that we trust Him, but do our actions show that? If we truly trust Him, then why are we worrying? As I mentioned before, I used to have a strong habit of worry. I would wake up worrying about things from yesterday, or worry about if I would be able to handle things today, and then worry about the future. It caused unneeded anxiety and stress which robbed me of peace and the energy to calmly go about my day. I realized that if I said that I believed God, and that He was worthy of my trust, then I couldn't keep on excusing my habit of worrying. I either trusted God, or I didn't. Were their things in my life and my family's life that I couldn't control? Of course, but worrying about them had not helped, it had actually made things worse.

I had to keep remembering Philippians 4:6-7, "Be anxious for nothing, but in everything by prayer and supplication with thanksgiving let your requests be made known to God. And the peace of God, which surpasses all comprehension, shall guard your hearts and your minds in Christ Jesus."

I set about relinquishing my worries in prayer to the Lord. I cannot say that there were immediate results. I had indulged my worry habit for a very long time. As a mom I had made excuses for why I should be worried about my kids or other family members or friends. But I couldn't reconcile that it was okay to worry and also say that I trusted God completely at the same time. So, I stopped justifying my worrying and started the process of relinquishing it to God every time it came up. And boy did it come up a lot!! Each time I recognized it, I took my worry to the Lord and laid my burdens down with Him. If I found myself worrying again, I repeated the process, not allowing any excuses or justifications for my anxiety.

You might be thinking that worry helps you to pray for others or take action or reach out to them and help them in some way. I asked the Lord to take all my worries and burdens and give me rest. I was trying to live in Matthew 11:28-30, "Come to Me, all who are weary and heavy-laden, and I will give you rest. Take My yoke upon you and learn from Me, for I am gentle and humble in heart, and you shall find rest for your souls. For My yoke is easy and My burden is light."

The portion of the burden He wants me to carry is light, with His help. As I asked the Lord to carry my burdens, I asked Him to leave me with enough of it to remember to pray for people and reach out to them, or to feel enough of what they were feeling so that I could be compassionate and come alongside them the way He intended. And the interesting thing is that He freed me to regard people as those whom He wants me to love, not to anticipate the burdens they might bring.

It took a while, and the change in my heart and mind was slow at first, but the Lord helped me to persevere. I can truly say now that I do not have a habit of worrying anymore. I can certainly worry about something when things happen, especially to my loved ones, but I do not have the habit of worrying at all. And I know where to go for help in my times of need. He is the strong and wise One. He knows how to answer our needs and provide for us in ways we can't imagine. How much calmer and at peace is my heart and mind, and how much more am I able to walk in thankfulness and trust, giving glory where it belongs, to my faithful burden bearer.

The prayer of relinquishment is also extremely valuable when it comes to parenting. Being a parent is such a daunting, challenging, rewarding job. We must be diligent, consistent, constantly teaching, molding, mentoring, planning, loving, disciplining, restoring. The Lord helps give me His wisdom and strength which I need so much. Each child is unique and totally different than the next. What works with one often does not work with the other. We have raised our own biological children, raised adopted children, had foster children and been a shelter home for runaways for our county. As parents, or responsible adults, we are called to build truth into their lives, but ultimately, we cannot reach in and make their choices for them.

Some parents have tried to manage their children's lives even when they became adults. This is rarely productive and usually impedes their ability to take responsibility for themselves, or it can alienate them from wanting their parents in their lives at all. Most adult children want the freedom to decide things for themselves and need the opportunity to make decisions and even mistakes. Most of us certainly made our share of mistakes when we were young adults.

The prayer of relinquishment comes into play in several ways in parenting. One of my children was extremely strong willed. From the age of 11 months until about 11 years old there were significant struggles with anger over who was in charge and basic issues of lack of obedience and respect. Rather than escalating the conflict by meeting force with force, the Lord had to teach me to relinquish the situation to Him day by day, sometimes minute by minute. It was difficult at first, but I built in ways for my child to take a time out and for me to do the same in order to de-escalate the situation. Then we could actually deal with the problem at hand and address the child's heart in the right way, rather than both of us having strong emotions. Strong willed children are usually astute about pushing every button their parent has. When the parent reacts with emotion, strong willed children often think the parent has the problem, rather than face their own part in the situation. As we were able to create time-outs, I would go into my room to pray. I relinquished the situation and the child into God's hands, asking for His wisdom and strength and peace. He gave me the calm I needed to put things in place and to address the heart of the matter with the child. He also reminded me that often in my life He has grace with me, forgives me, restores me, and gives me fresh starts. It was very important that I do the same with my child. Strong willed children often are unable to control themselves and it can take a long time and a lot of consistency to help them with this process.

After this child was grown, they told me that the grace which was given to them to enable them to have fresh starts was so important. It gave them hope and a chance to start over in new ways. Eventually the outbursts became fewer, and around the age of 11 this child surrendered their heart to follow God in more mature and obedient ways. They had believed in God as their Savior some years before, but there was an obvious change in their life and their actions as they submitted themselves to the Lord. There were at times outbursts of will, but they were followed by apologies and recognition of the need to respect us as parents. I was shocked the first time this happened, but so grateful that the Lord had worked in my child's life and heart to make these choices on their own.

Similarly, we cannot change the heart of our adult children. However, we can relinquish them to the Lord and ask for Him to continue to work in their lives. As we pray for them and give them to the Lord, He is free to work and to accomplish His good purposes. He can give us wisdom with our interactions with them as adults, including what to say to them and what not to say. It is similar with our family and friends. We can often pray for them and with them at their point of need, demonstrating compassion and caring and helping where we can. But ultimately what they need much of the time is to go to Him. We cannot own their choices, but we can place them into the hand of God for Him to work in their lives in His way and according to His timing. And the Lord directs us in how He wants us to help them and love them.

In the chapter on honesty and humility I have written about my past and the pain I carried from some things in my life. I was severely abused, lost relationships, experienced hurt and pain from others and from a lack of belonging. The Lord longs to set us free. By the Holy Spirit's direction, I wrote down all of the things which were causing me pain from my past. The prayer of relinquishment was key to the Lord setting me free. I had to be willing to be made well and whole. I had to be willing to really let go of these things and put them into the hands of God. As I relinquished them to His keeping, one by one, the pain was healed and did not return. I didn't know that was possible.

I have prayed with others who wanted to be set free. At times, the Lord can heal multiple things at one time, when the person is willing to truly let go of them and trust the Lord to take them and let themselves be loved by the Lord. At other times it is a gradual step by step process, as they come to terms with accepting and truly relinquishing the hurts they carry. Sometimes they need to talk to the Lord about forgiving someone who has hurt them. He can help us to do that. It is interesting that emotional pain is something we carry so very close to ourselves. At times it has almost become a companion, and strong emotions can often color our memories and make them intense. Sometimes it is almost hard to let go of them, because we fear we will lose part of ourselves or others.

Caring for my husband for 25 years was wrapped up with his suffering and limitations. One way of showing love to him was caring for his body, especially after his stroke, helping him get dressed, to the bathroom, cleaned up, settled in his chair, bringing him food and drink. As his body grew weaker this took a toll on all of us who were his caregivers. Our muscles, tendons and backs were often strained, yet we gladly took care of his needs. When the Lord took him home to heaven, I knew he was now rejoicing and completely well again. I rejoiced in that, even while I faced a huge loss and resulting sadness. The Lord promised to be faithful to me and to be with me. A few weeks later He asked me to let go of the burden I carried for so many years of caring for my husband and to walk out of the "valley of the shadow" and back into life. I didn't know how to do that. In my mind, caring for John was equal to loving him, even though it came at a sacrifice. The Lord helped me to relinquish those things. I realized that I could still love John and yet let go of the burden I had carried for so long of caring for him, including releasing my pain which had come from sharing in the suffering that he had endured day after day. When I relinquished it all to the Lord, He set me free. He called me to participate in new ministries, and I found that I had new energy and a renewed emotional openness to deeply care about all of the people around me.

If you have carried pain or hurt from your past, ask the Holy Spirit to work in you to prepare you to relinquish it. This is not the same as laying things down at His feet, and then taking them back again with you. Relinquishment means opening up your hands and heart and truly letting it go completely into His keeping. When you do that by a choice of your will, the Lord takes it as a settled transaction. He will work in you to heal you and set you free to walk in joy with Him. He may also show you that the pain and hurt you carried for so long caused you to develop patterns of fear or insecurity or anger in your life. Or perhaps you built up your defenses in order to protect yourself from others or from things you feared or were hurt by in the past. These things may even be affecting how you relate to other people today. It will be impossible to be completely free and emotionally healthy and whole unless you allow the Lord to heal you in these areas. He can teach you how to walk with a newness of life. He has done it in my life. There are so many Scriptures which talk about the purposes He has for us. And He has the power to heal, restore, and make new.

Colossians 3:1-3 "Therefore, if you have been raised up with Christ, keep seeking the things above, where Christ is, seated at the right hand of God. Set your mind on the things above, not on the things that are on earth. For you have died and your life is hidden with Christ in God."

Philippians 1:6 "For I am confident of this very thing, that He who began a good work in you will perfect it until the day of Christ Jesus."

Psalm 23:1-3 "The Lord is my shepherd, I shall not want. He makes me lie down in green pastures; He leads me beside quiet waters, He restores my soul."

John 8:31-32 "So Jesus was saying to those Jews who had believed Him, 'If you continue in My word then you are truly disciples of Mine; and you shall know the truth and the truth will make you free.'"

Ephesians 3:16-20 "That He would grant you, according to the riches of His glory, to be strengthened with power through His Spirit in the inner man; so that Christ may dwell in your hearts through faith; and that you being rooted and grounded in love, may be able to comprehend with all the saints what is the breadth and length and height and depth and to know the love of Christ which surpasses knowledge, that you may be filled up to all the fullness of God."

The prayer of relinquishment is key in the area of our plans, our goals, and our seeking of direction. I have heard many speakers and read a number of authors who talk about finding the will of God. It is almost like you are looking for one particular piece of guidance from the Lord, and then you plan on taking that and running off in the direction you need to go. The Scriptures actually talk a lot about the will of God. There are many, many verses which tell us that God's will for us is to obey Him, follow Him, be thankful, love others, etc. I have sought the Lord many times for direction. I used to treat Him as a vending machine in which I put in my prayers and hoped to get my answer so I could run off and accomplish what I needed to do, usually by my own power. What a sad idea of trying to do God's will. His plan is so much better. Do we need direction? Of course, we do. We are not very wise and do not know the future, and often we don't see where God is working or what direction He wants us to head. We often don't pay attention to where God would like us to invest in the lives around us. We are so short sighted and self-centered. As we bring our questions and need for direction and guidance to our Heavenly Father, His plan is to prepare us and walk with us through each moment and each day. As we abide with Him, we will be where He wants us, doing exactly what we should be doing by His power, strength, and wisdom each moment. As we obey and walk with Him, we experience ongoing guidance and the ability to walk with Him and bless others. We find that He orchestrates divine appointments and leads us where He wants us.

I have often been guilty of wanting to run ahead of Him. When He would share some guidance with me, I would get organized, make my lists of things I needed to accomplish and eventually pat myself on the back when I could check the things off of my list. We feel good about ourselves when we look at what we have achieved. Often, I have achieved far less of value than I think. Oh, I may have accomplished a lot of tasks, but whose heart did I connect with that day? In fact, did I even make time to really talk with people who came into my path, or did I shorten that encounter so I could get back to my priorities? Which do you think was God's priority? I started realizing that I was missing one of the most important things of the day, by not paying attention to who God was bringing my way. I started lifting my checklist to the Lord so that He could show me what were His priorities for the day. And this was even during a time when I had a very busy job as a high-level manager. He always knows best. I found that as I relinquished my day to Him, I was not behind in my job, quite the contrary. Things would come to my mind which I needed to prepare beforehand, right before they were needed. Or I would be given wisdom on how to handle something in a different way than anyone had done before. I can't claim the credit. He was sharing His wisdom with me as I realized my need for it and relinquished my day and my problems to Him.

I remember vividly how the Lord taught me about running ahead of Him. Early during John's illness, he was still able to work. His company shut down, so he found work in a different state. We moved, and every morning I would take a walk with the Lord to spend time with Him and seek His direction in this new location. One day the Holy Spirit asked me to take our dog on the walk with me. I reminded Him that the dog was distracting and not broken to the leash well, and I didn't want to take him. The still small voice told me again to take the dog with me. I obeyed and off we went. The walk wound through the neighborhood and then followed a path beside a lake. As expected, the dog was distracted and wanted to run in the direction of the lake where geese were flying in and landing on the water. The dog pulled this way and that way, tugging me along the path in different directions. I felt justified in my earlier thoughts about not bringing him, until a still small voice interrupted my thinking. He said, "This is how you are with Me. You often run ahead in one direction or another, leaving my side and not walking with Me. You miss so much by doing that." I have never forgotten this vivid lesson.

I wish I could say I never ran ahead of the Lord again, but it was a learning process for me. I still have that tendency. I hear from the Lord and get excited and want to start doing things, but now I look up sheepishly and the Lord and I laugh about my tendencies, and I try to remain right by His side. I am so glad He is patient with me!! He is so amazing to walk with and talk with. He opens up my eyes to see things and people right in front of me which I could easily miss if I was filled up with my own plans. The prayer of relinquishment is key to being able to walk tenderly moment by moment with Him. I am amazed at the things He has helped me to accomplish and the people whom I have been able to share with when I trust everything to Him day by day. Relinquishment has become a huge blessing, for it invites God to work in my heart and in my life and unites me with the purposes and the heart of God.

CHAPTER 5

THE LOVE OF GOD

The love of God is at the heart of our relationship with Him. You could write enough books to fill a library and still not completely cover the truth of the immensity of His love. When I think of how utterly powerful and great our God is, I am so profoundly grateful that He is a loving God and that He is good, faithful, and true. His Word is full of His lovingkindness toward us and His longsuffering patience. He determined to redeem and restore us and bring us back to Himself into a close, intimate relationship that only He could have orchestrated.

You can see His love in the garden of Eden. He took such great care in the creation of man, breathing life into him, providing for him. He created Eve to come alongside Adam because He wanted Adam to have a loving partner. There was wonderful provision in the garden. If they had heeded His warning, it would have spared them so much. And when they transgressed and realized their sin and nakedness, He covered them. Were there consequences for their sin? There always are. Without the school of consequences how would we possibly learn things of value, how would sinners seek for a Savior, realize their need for God and the truth of His Word?

Even from the beginning God promised a Savior. Despite men's sinful choices, over and over God saved a remnant who turned to Him in faith and walked obediently with Him. He established a people for His own possession. He saved and protected them through Joseph in the land of Egypt during years of famine. Eventually God delivered them out of Egypt through signs and wonders accomplished in God's power and announced by Moses and Aaron to Pharaoh. God gave the new nation rules to live by and promises of the land He would provide for them. Despite their unfaithfulness, He remained faithful to His promises. After they were established in the land as a nation, they were often unfaithful to God. Through the ages God sent prophets to talk to the people to turn them back from their sin to the living God. Time and again He heard their cries and rescued them. Israel ultimately became a divided kingdom, and as they continued to pursue other gods, they were eventually conquered and dispersed. But God kept His promise to bring them back into the land and to once again call them His people. Through His great mercy He established them as a nation once more. Only a loving God would then send His very own Son, the promised Savior, born humbly in a manger, announced to shepherds, sought out by wise men.

If all we knew about God's love was summed up in Jesus and His willing sacrifice for us, it would be enough. Jesus demonstrated compassion on the people, healing many. He taught astonishing truths which could liberate them from oppression into the freedom of knowing they had a heavenly Father who cared for them. So many times, He displayed God's great mercy and taught the people about God's desire to deliver them from fear and from anxiety over the future. He talked to them about the willingness of God to draw them near and to offer them eternal life if they would believe. Jesus demonstrated such a close union with His Father, doing only the things which He knew the Father wanted Him to do.

John 8:28-29 "So Jesus said, 'When you lift up the Son of Man, then you will know that I am He, and I do nothing on My own initiative, but I speak these things as the Father taught Me. And He who sent Me is with Me; He has not left Me alone, for I always do the things that are pleasing to Him."'

In the face of impending torture and great suffering, Jesus prayed with great earnestness in the garden of Gethsemane. Who would not want to avoid the fate that was in front of Him? Yet He trusted so much in the Father's great plan that He was willing to be the sacrifice that God had determined must be given in order to redeem us all. That picture alone encapsulates the heart of God who sacrificed His own beloved Son for sinful men in order to restore us to Himself and draw us near.

Romans 8:32 "He who did not spare His own Son, but delivered Him over for us all, how will He not also with Him freely give us all things?"

Romans 5:8 "But God demonstrates His own love toward us, in that while we were yet sinners, Christ died for us."

And then we move to the foot of the cross. We scarcely dare gaze on Jesus as his body hung on the cross enduring such agony. He did not defend Himself when questioned and judged, but willingly set Himself to follow the Father's plan through to the end. But wait, there is even more! As He hangs there surrounded by sinful and ignorant men who have purposed to torture Him and kill Him, He utters words that are hardly believable from an innocent man accused, beaten, and condemned to die, "Father forgive them for they do not know what they are doing" (Luke 23:34.)

Jesus was willing even during that terrible time of suffering, to be our Savior, to rescue us and not Himself! Our heavenly Father was willing to forgive us, which was

His purpose in sending His Son. The Holy Spirit was willing to dwell with us, so that if we believe and trust in Jesus, God's Spirit could make us come alive unto God, and we would know wonderful fellowship with Him. What a stunningly beautiful plan almost beyond our comprehension of what true sacrificial love means.

Those of us who understand and believe, stand in great wonder at the cross. As sinful people we could never have saved ourselves. On our own we would not have known God. He did it all so that He could bring us to Himself. And it doesn't end at the cross. As the Holy Spirit reminded me recently, Jesus did not die at the cross so that we would know a little about His love, or to give us a small deliverance. Great is His love and power toward those who believe.

Ephesians 1:18-19 says, "I pray that the eyes of your heart may be enlightened, so that you will know what is the hope of His calling, what are the riches of the glory of His inheritance in the saints, and what is the surpassing greatness of His power toward us who believe."

Romans 5:5 "And hope does not disappoint, because the love of God has been poured out within our hearts through the Holy Spirit who was given to us."

Incredibly the loving plan from the heart of God included making us His beloved children. Jesus talked with His followers to help them understand that He wanted them to have an intimate relationship with the Father, like His. If we love Him and obey Him, the Father and the Son would abide with us. The beauty of that type of relationship is often lost on us. Most of the time we want to know what we need to do, check the right boxes, and go about our life under our own lordship. We settle for so little of what He intended. God purposed far more for us.

In His great love, He never intended for us to walk alone. In fact, He promised never to leave us or abandon us. We are only alone if we choose not to walk in fellowship with Him. His intention was for us to abide in Him, in a wonderfully loving relationship. He intended to set us free from so many things like fear, anxiety, bondage to sin. He wants to provide us with the fruits of His Spirit. He is willing to share with us part of who He is, which enables us to know joy, peace, forgiveness, gentleness, faithfulness, wisdom, strength. And He provides in such amazing ways when we trust Him.

I have shared before about how He very specifically brought encouragement to me in the ICU waiting room, and how He answered my cries of distress by providing His deep peace. He has also been an incredible provider. My husband had a good job, but as his serious brain condition progressed there were a number of times when he could not work and had to take disability leaves from his job. Disability pay was not sufficient for our family, and we exhausted all of our savings and retirement accounts over time. I had not worked for a while because I was so involved in taking John to medical appointments and sometimes ER visits. His brain condition was not always stable, and there were times when he was not lucid. The children were now teenagers and were helping with his care, so I thought of seeking part time work.

I found an office about 10 miles from my home which needed a part time administrative worker. When I applied, they gave me a series of tasks to determine my suitability for the position. They became so confident in my abilities, that they expanded the job to include flying to airports around California to meet with professional people working for the state and document their airport meetings.

I was to be the scribe for these high-level committee meetings and report back all of the details and then send them out to everyone. They also wanted to increase the hours of the job. When they called me and offered me the position, they were excited about the possibilities. I was overwhelmed.

I went for a walk and talked with the Lord at length about it. It was one thing to be 10 minutes away from home and to be able to come back if needed in an emergency. It was totally another to be working more hours each day at a much greater distance and not be accessible to my family. We had asked the Lord to provide for us. I talked to the Lord and said that the last thing I wanted to do was to despise an opportunity of His provision, if this is what He intended. However, I was a wife and mother first and foremost. I didn't feel comfortable taking the job. I didn't have to give my answer about accepting the position until the next morning. I prayed, offering for the Lord to work in my mind and heart if He was choosing this job opportunity for me. I didn't want to disappoint the Lord in any way. I continued to pray during the night, but the next morning I still felt that my primary responsibility was to be available to care for my family. I called and reluctantly turned down the job even though it would have made me feel better about our financial security.

I placed our financial needs in the hands of the Lord. Two days later I was at church teaching a Bible study to teenage girls. There was a knock at the door and the Children's Education Director for our church asked to speak with me. I had worked with her in children's ministries for a number of years. She told me she was going to return to her job as a schoolteacher. She had recommended to the church elders that I should become the next Children's Education Director. It would be a part time paid position. She said that the elders wanted to offer me the job with one condition. They knew of our family's situation, so they wanted me to work the job around my family's needs. I was stunned. I would be able to work doing a job I already loved, receive pay that my family could definitely use, and take care of my family's needs at the same time. My heart was rejoicing at the loving provision that the Lord had planned.

I could tell many more stories of His provision for us through the years. Eventually years later as John became permanently disabled, the Lord not only provided a career for me, but He put me in positions of leadership which I would never have expected. As my work challenges grew, He was always there to give me the daily wisdom I needed and the courage to take on new opportunities. He gave me grace to reach out to others that I worked with sharing about His truth and how much He cared for them. When we know His great love for us, we become channels of that love so that others can see Him and come to know Him.

I have shared in other chapters how the Lord set me free from my pain of the past, and from fears that I had carried for years. He delivered me from the habit of worrying and being overcome with anxiety, and He replaced those things with trust and confidence in His love and His goodness. At first when I sought Him out, it was often to get guidance and reassurance during difficult times. But as I came to know Him it was not His voice of guidance which I sought, but His very presence in my life and in my heart. His Spirit always lives to draw us nearer to our God in a very close and loving relationship.

I still seek Him, but it is less about what He can give than just to spend time with Him. He IS love. The Lord loves us. Think about what that means for a moment. The LORD loves us. The God and Creator of all we see is the One who has done everything to draw us near to Himself. The Lord LOVES us. His love is full of grace and truth, and it is more immense than we can possibly understand. The Lord loves US. He is not willing that any should perish, far from it, He provided everything possible to deliver us. Although we are sinful people, He removes our sin, covers us with His righteousness, and gives us eternal life so that we can be where He is. He lavishes us with His grace.

Ephesians 1:7-8 "In Him we have redemption through His blood, the forgiveness of our trespasses according to the riches of His grace which He lavished on us."

God has done so many things in my life. He provided the sacrifice of my Savior so that He could forgive my sins. He put me into an intimate relationship with Him where I can call Him, "Abba, Father." I have become His child, welcomed into the throne room of God in a close relationship. I am covered with the righteousness of Christ so that I can approach the Holy One with confidence and great joy. I am beloved. I have been able to teach others about His love and His ability to set us free. I have certainly experienced many times His loving care and His loving presence. Yet the Lord had more to teach me about His love.

In my position as a manager in healthcare I was expected to go to at least one national conference a year. This was important as it would give me the opportunity to learn from great speakers, as well as collaborate with other managers from across the nation to work on solutions for complicated problems. I had become part of a network of managers around the country. We shared and worked on very complex issues together. When I would go to these conferences, I had to arrange care for my husband while I was away. Sometimes I would talk with the Lord and receive His guidance to add a day or part of a day at the beginning or the end of the conference to spend with Him as a spiritual retreat.

It was 2019, and I needed to go to Chicago to the national conference in June. When I talked about it with the Lord, I was startled to hear that I needed to spend three days before the conference on a spiritual retreat with Him. I received clear confirmation and was able to work out all of the arrangements fairly easily. There were very detailed instructions about flying to Montana on my way to Chicago, and then driving to a cabin in the woods on a ranch in Wyoming. To get there I would need to fly into one of two airports in Montana, either Billings or Bozeman. The ranch was located south in Wyoming, right between the airports which both had highways connecting to it which ran through the mountains. I looked at the flight schedules for non-stop flights to Montana and further connections on to Chicago. Bozeman seemed to clearly be the better choice for flights. I lifted a prayer for confirmation. I heard the quiet voice of the Spirit say that I needed to fly into Billings. Do you ever find yourself "reminding" the Almighty of things, as if He doesn't know already? I pointed out that the connections were better at the Bozeman airport. His voice again said with surety that I needed to fly into Billings. So, I booked the trip to Billings. I was a little concerned about spending money for myself on this trip, the additional flight cost, the rental car, the cabin. Extra money had been provided unexpectedly just before this, so I set myself to obey what I believed the Lord wanted me to do.

On the plane I was studying the Word of God and a Bible study which spoke about the love of God. When I got the rental car, I started driving into Wyoming. I had checked all the roads and all conditions were shown as favorable. I had brought three music CDs with me, but the first two wouldn't play in the car at all (they did later.) The third CD was the only one that would play. The songs on that CD were about the love of God and the words and music ministered to my heart. I was part way into Wyoming and was looking forward to driving through some scenic territory through the Beartooth Mountains. Just before I got there, I saw a flashing sign. The road was closed due to high winds and drifting snow. I needed to take a detour. On the highway coming from Billings, this meant a detour of 20 minutes. The same road was closed from the Bozeman side and would have meant a detour of 6 hours. The Lord certainly had my full attention, and I was praising His name.

I was a little disappointed at missing the scenic route until I turned from the detour onto the highway I needed to get to the ranch. The road opened up to a magnificent vista. I pulled the car over and stopped in wonder. Snowcapped mountains filled 180 degrees of my view. A meadow opened up before me which rose and then fell into valleys which were covered with evergreen forests. A majestic escarpment was to my left which had layers of red and yellow rock which fell steeply to the valley floor. I was thanking God for His wonderful, creative power.

Then the Lord asked me to notice a little scraggly baby pine which was on the top of the first rise closest to me. He told me that all I knew of His love was this little scraggly pine, when He had mountains and valleys and vast forests which I had not explored. He gave me a mental picture of a feast which He had prepared. It was a very long table wonderfully spread with beautiful dishes and all types of food. This is the banquet that He loves to prepare for His children, to lavish them with His love. He showed me that I was not sitting at it. I was only content to pick up morsels which had fallen from the table. I did not consider myself worthy to have a full measure of His love.

I was humbled by the revelations. I have known His great grace, His forgiveness, His provision, His comfort. But I knew that I had not experienced the fullness of how much He loves me. How could I teach about it unless I understood it better? I sensed that the Lord wanted to teach me very personal things during our three days together. I drove on thoughtfully and checked in at the ranch. The cabin was very secluded in the woods, heated by a wood stove which I needed to keep feeding in order to stay warm. The overwhelming sound which filled my ears was that of the roaring river 25 feet from my cabin door. Due to the snowmelt in the mountains, this fork of the Yellowstone River was in flood stage. The water was pouring down this canyon, tumbling and rushing over anything in its path. I won't go into all of the details of what God was teaching me through His Word and His Spirit, but a couple of things stood out.

The next day after studying Scriptures about His love, He asked me to walk to a spot on the riverbank. The river curved at just that spot. As I stood there it looked like the water was all rushing right at me, but then at the last minute it curved and roared past. At my feet was a little rivulet of water which ran in a small curve around the bank. The Lord showed me that up to now I had believed that because of the sacrifice of Jesus, I could receive forgiveness and a little bit of God's love like this little rivulet of water. He reminded me of some memories of my past where I had been told I was not worthy, unless I earned approval by being good. I had not realized this still had an effect on me. The Lord asked me to look up. He said that His love was like this rushing stream, vast and everflowing from His throne room through the cross to me.

The immensity and the generosity of the Lord's love overwhelmed me. I almost fell to my knees. I cried out that I was not worthy. The Lord had forgiven my sins, but there were still times when I failed Him or didn't obey Him right away. He said lovingly, "And I still love you." I cried out that sometimes I didn't love people as much as I should. He said in a tender voice, "And I still love you." All of the things I had tried to accomplish in my own power in order to be worthy or pleasing to others or to God were floating away on the breeze that was blowing. None of those things mattered at all. The Lord God of heaven and earth loved me with an overwhelming love that had no end. The Lord said gently, "Let Me love you."

It is hard to describe how fundamentally life changing this was for me. From that moment on those words have come to me often, "Let Me love you." Now if I am put in a position (especially in a public setting) where in times past I would have tried to meet everyone's expectations or try to prove my worth in some way, I hear those words again. I relax and know that I am thoroughly and completely loved by my King.

Why did I not know this sooner? The Lord knows when we are ready to receive truth. And He knew what was going to happen in the next 2 years, what He was going to ask of me, and what I was going to walk through. His precise timing was so valuable, and His love continues to fill my life with great joy. Now I KNOW His love and it doesn't depend on me, He is the one that matters most. He is incredibly patient with me.

The three days in Wyoming were amazing. I would have given everything I owned to be there. I was delayed at the airport when traveling to Chicago. I arrived at the first large session of the conference with five minutes to spare. I didn't know that my manager would in a few minutes hand me the microphone to answer a question from the moderator, to give information to the whole assembly. But my heart was at rest, and I was able to speak of changes and solutions we had found in our programs. This enabled me to have some very creative conversations over the next few days with other managers.

On Friday morning I was eating in my room when the Lord asked me to go downstairs and draw near to someone I had just met at the conference. He said she would be arriving to eat breakfast. I didn't know if she was a believer or not. When I obeyed, this woman welcomed me, and we had a wonderful conversation about the Lord. She was going through immense difficulties in her personal life. She had felt the Lord wanted her to come to the conference, and He had providentially provided the funding for her when she had thought it was not possible. When I told her the Lord had sent me to her, with tears she said how much that encouraged her. She needed confirmation of the Lord's love for her.

For the next several months we stayed in contact and prayed together. About a month later, the Lord asked me to tell her that she was not alone, He knew all about her life, and He would be with her. She cried at those words because at that exact time she felt like she was all alone and that no one cared. She was able to lead her two children to trust in what God had for them and walk through her difficulties with the Lord's help.

The Lord is so personal and cares so deeply. There have been times when I should have encouraged someone, and I didn't. I have needed to ask for His forgiveness. It is likely that He sent someone else to help them instead of me. I have tried to learn from those times that my list of things to do is never more important than the heart of the person God is bringing my way. Are there people who are particularly challenging in your life? God was also teaching me that challenging people are not burdens. Some of the things they do may be burdensome, but they are people loved by God. They need to be treated with love and mercy. Doesn't God treat us that way, even though we have done nothing to deserve it?

In 2019 the Lord began to ask me to come walk with Him on my lunch hour. We had very tender conversations together. He told me that things were going to get worse for my husband, but that He would be with us. He also began to talk about a new direction for our lives that would involve retiring from my job in June of 2021 and moving about 2 hours away. I "reminded" Him that I had planned on working a few more years to earn more for retirement, and that I was also caring for my mother and helping my sister who was disabled. They both lived just a mile from me. How could I move? He told me gently that my mother would be with Him by then, and He would take care of my sister. My mother was not even ill at that time, but 6 months later she developed some symptoms suddenly. She only remained with us for another 6 weeks before departing for her heavenly home. A few months later my sister felt called by God to move back to be closer to her children and grandchildren.

The Lord was confirming His directions in so many ways. I gave my retirement notice of June 2021 to my workplace, and they started looking for a replacement. Then the Lord told me that my husband would be with Him before I retired! I had placed John into the Lord's hands for the last 25 years of his illness. I knew that things could change at any time and had witnessed his progressive decline after his stroke in 2013. I walked and talked a lot with the Lord, who helped me as I worked through my deep sadness and the grieving process, alone with Him. I asked Him to give me the strength to continue to lovingly care for John for all of his remaining days on earth.

I took pains to carefully obey every detail that the Lord shared with me. It became clear that the Lord was calling me into a ministry opportunity as administrator of a Christian school in a city 2 hours away. In my past I had taught for 12 years and worked at an elementary school in administration for a few years. I had also worked as an administrator in my current job in healthcare for almost 15 years. I found out that the current administrator of the Christian school had given notice that her last day would be in June of 2021! On my first house hunting trip I found a house for us. That same weekend I met with the School Board. Within a couple of months, they officially invited me to become the new administrator starting in July of 2021. We sold our house and moved to a new city and to our new house. I finished up my job in healthcare by Zoom, training a new manager. The faithfulness of God and His incredibly detailed provision for us were so apparent.

About 2 months after our move John had a serious event involving brain trauma. He was not stable and did not recognize any of us, and he was airlifted to another hospital. Thankfully within 4 days he once again knew who we were, but his health and even his mind would never be quite the same. The Lord gave me the courage to put everything in place to care for him and get him home, despite the hospital's insistence that we put him in a skilled nursing facility.

We had wonderful family times with him for two weeks. On the day before my retirement was official, he passed away gently. It was the day I had dreaded for so long, for my husband and best friend was gone. Yet on the day of his burial, the Lord asked me to get up early and come outside with Him. I sat on my patio gazing at the stars and the moon. The Lord told me that just as He continues to keep the world in orbit and the stars and moon continue to shine at night, He would be faithful to me. He said that the moon and stars would pass away before His love for me would pass away.

God was so gentle and loving with each one of us in the family. Our daughter who lived far away was already there with us, and she helped me immensely to care for John in his last days. We were all able to get together and celebrate the life of this courageous and loving man who had been such an integral part of all of our lives. He fought through limitations, great pain and weakness, anger at his condition, and ultimately submission to receiving help from others for every single need of his life. He worked through all of those things and continued to love and support every one of us. We had been so blessed by his life. Now he was completely well and with the Lord. The Lord told me that He would take care of John now.

The Lord wants to come alongside every one of us. He loves us and walks with us in such tender ways. Regardless of our challenges, if they are placed into His hands, He brings good. He wants us to abide with Him. He wants to free us so that we know how much He loves us and how much we can love others.

When we make mistakes or don't obey Him, as we turn to Him, He is willing to forgive and restore us right back to His side. He is the Faithful One, even when we aren't. He wants to send us to help and encourage others. That is what love is all about. He loves us so completely, and we get to love Him back.

Is there anything standing in the way of your realizing just how much He loves you? If there is, ask Him to show you what that is. Surrender it into His keeping so that you will know His immense love for you. Some people have not had a faithful father on earth, and they have a tough time relating to their Father in heaven. Picture the type of Dad which you should have had. That is what God intended for fathers to be. Know that God the Father is full of love for His children. He does not remove all of our suffering. They are part of the era we live in caused by sin. To remove all suffering would be to remove all sinful people, us included. But He walks with us through it all if we invite Him into it.

Are you spending time getting to know Him better? I am convinced that He wants to talk to us much more than we want to listen. Do you remember the initial excitement of making special times to spend with someone you loved? Make time to spend with Him. Open yourself up to receiving His love.

Listen to His Words, both in writing and the ones He speaks to you. Obey Him. He is the Creator; He has a thousand ways to tell us things. His spoken word will never contradict His written Word. You will get better in time recognizing not only the voice of your Shepherd but His presence in your life. If you make mistakes in this pursuit, then bring that to Him also. Don't turn away from a loving walk with your Creator God who loves you so much. Allow His love to fill you up so that you can love others like He does.

Let Him love you.

Ephesians 3:14-19 "For this reason I bow my knees before the Father, from whom every family in heaven and on earth derives its name, that He would grant you, according to the riches of His glory, to be strengthened with power through His Spirit in the inner man, so that Christ may dwell in your hearts through faith; and that you, being rooted and grounded in love, may be able to comprehend with all the saints what is the breadth and length and height and depth, and to know the love of Christ which surpasses knowledge, that you may be filled up to all the fullness of God."

CHAPTER 6

FINDING HIM

Deuteronomy 4:29 "But from there you will seek the Lord your God, and you will find Him if you search for Him with all your heart and all your soul."

Psalm 14:2 "The LORD has looked down from heaven upon the sons of men to see if there are any who understand, who seek after God."

The Scriptures are full of references which urge us to seek the Lord our God. The Lord said in Jeremiah 29:13 that if we would seek Him with all our heart, we would find Him. Proverbs 8:17 says the same, as well as verses in the gospels that say that the one who seeks will find, to the one who knocks it will be opened. We don't find what we are looking for unless we actually look for it. What are you looking for? What are you seeking? People seek long and hard to find treasures on this earth. They rejoice greatly when they find them. What do you count as your treasure? What would thrill your soul if you found it? How long would your treasure last? Would it endure for a brief time or for a while? Would it endure for a lifetime or an eternity?

We seek after many things, but the most precious treasure by far is a relationship with the Almighty God who created us. Throughout the Scriptures He displays His Father's heart and His longing for us to draw near to Him as His beloved children. As believers we have an initial knowledge of our God and our Savior, with the removal of our sins and the resulting freedom to walk clothed in His righteousness. That is an amazing reality that we have been offered through the finished work of the cross. Jesus promised that if we would love Him and keep His Word, that the Father and the Son would dwell with us.

John 14:23 "Jesus answered and said to him, 'If anyone loves Me, he will keep My Word; and My Father will love him, and We will come to him and make Our abode with him.'"

What would you give in order to find a close, intimate walk with God, to walk and talk with Him, to experience His love completely and fully, to be free to live life abundantly? We know that as believers we have received His Holy Spirit which has made us alive to God spiritually. We can now worship God in Spirit and truth. As we draw near to Him in faith, He promises to draw near to us (James 4:8.)

During the years that my parents were missionaries, they met a 21-year-old girl whose family had recently immigrated from an Eastern nation. She was a college student who was eager to learn many things. She started attending our church, and she became excited to study the Bible to learn more about Christ. Within a few months she had taken the step of putting her trust in Christ. She understood that by Christ's death on the cross and His resurrection, her sins could be forgiven, and she could have new life, a new relationship as a child of God. When she told her family about her new faith, at first they were happy for her. They told her she could bring a symbol of the cross and add it to the wall in their home where their religious icons were hanging. That way they could include this new god in their worship of their many gods. The girl bravely and respectfully spoke up and said that the God she worshipped and trusted was the only true God. She shared that she had learned and come to believe what Jesus said, that He was the way, the truth, and the life and that no one comes to Father God except through Jesus (John 14:6.) When she kept insisting on these truths, the parents grew exceedingly upset. Before the evening was over, they told her that if she insisted on holding to her new beliefs, she would no longer be welcome in their house. Gathering a few of her belongings, the girl had to leave her family home. It seemed a terrible price to pay, but she had decided to follow Christ, and she would not turn back. He was her Savior and Lord. She found a home for a while with some people from the church. She rejoiced that she had found Christ, even though she was sad at the loss of her family. The family eventually restored their relationship with the girl, and God worked through her life in remarkable ways.

I wonder if in our Western culture, we don't make the same mistake which that Eastern family initially did by trying to add Christ to the other things we hold most dear. Are we sold out to seeking and finding our God with whole-hearted devotion? Or do we want Christ plus some of the idols in our lives? Do we want Christ and our comforts? Do we want Christ and our entertainment? Do we want Christ plus our position, power, prestige, play times, money, earthly treasures, all of our stuff? Many of these things are not bad in themselves, but they have taken on such huge importance in our lives that we wouldn't give them up if He asked us to. Are there sins which we have cozied up to and are aware of that we just "can't give up?"

Competing desires will pull us in opposite directions. You must let go of one to completely follow the other. You cannot fully grasp the things of this world and fully grasp

Christ. Which do you want to hold on to? What will you let go of? Which do you desire most?

Our Lord has saved us for heaven and eternity, and He gave everything for us. Are we fully His? Are we walking with Him as Lord and giving Him the right to ask us to fulfill His will here on earth? Are we seeking Him daily, even moment by moment? Do we seek His heart, seek what is important to Him, seek His mission, find out who He is and what His plans are for us?

2 Chronicles 16:9 says, "For the eyes of the LORD move to and fro throughout the earth that He may strongly support those whose heart is completely His."

Who is on the throne in our lives? Are we doing things in our own sufficiency, making our own plans, and carrying out our will or are we walking closely with Him? Are we yielded to Him so that His power flows through us? Do we experience the fruits of the Spirit in our lives? What are we pursuing? What are we investing in? What do we spend our time on? Do we trust in Him, or do we run to find our own solutions according to our own human "wisdom"? What have we been saved to? What is our heart occupied with? What are our thoughts full of?

If we could see and hear Him standing right in front of us, would we turn and follow Him and do what He asks of us, or would we turn away to our own plans? Do we want to know our Creator and be about the purposes He created us for? Do we want to encourage and love those He sends us to? What desires do we have? What desires are we pursuing? When we have a need or face trouble or trials, where do we turn? What are we trusting in, our own strength, our plans, our bank account, our problem-solving abilities, or do we trust and wait on our Almighty God to answer in ways that are different from the world's? His ways are beautiful and filled with grace.

Finding Him is not a destination, it is a journey walked with Him step by step. It is a relationship, and as we seek Him, He draws near to us so that we are walking heart to heart with the Holy and Faithful One. It becomes more important to us to build this sweet relationship with Him than to come to Him to withdraw what we need from His "bank account" or His storehouses, even though He provides that often. When you find Him there is sweet harmony together, there is unity, trust, laughter, honesty, humility, yieldedness, correction, new perspectives, guidance, and great love.

So what do we need to do to find Him? After you have believed in the saving grace of His Son, and the Holy Spirit has come to dwell in you, continue to seek Him and invite Him into every day. Have faith, trust Him, believe that He wants to walk closely with you.

Hebrews 11:6 "And without faith it is impossible to please Him, for he who comes to God must believe that He is and that He is a rewarder of those who seek Him."

Refine your desires, let the passion you have for many other things go. Desire to know Him above all else. Yield to Him seeking His desires for you. Do you think any good parent would want to harm their child? How much more does your heavenly Father work for good?

Matthew 7:11 "If you then, being evil, know how to give good gifts to your children, how much more will your Father who is in heaven give what is good to those who ask Him!"

Talk to Him at every opportunity. Read His Word and find out what He is like, and why He had the Scriptures written for your benefit. What are His desires for us?

Listen for His voice. When He talks it will be in line with His character and the Scriptures. One wonderful man of faith said that it is very difficult to hear the Lord's voice when we are filled with our own agenda. We are often looking more for His rubber stamp of approval on our plans than seeking Him and His ways. Lay down your own agenda. Surrender it completely to Him and truly listen to what He wants to share with you.

When He speaks, write it down immediately. I have found that when He tells me something, if I am not careful, I add words to it or put the message into a context of my own making. I may think it applies to one thing, and He may mean something else. Write it down as soon as possible in the exact way you heard Him say it. It will help you to look back on it and know that He spoke and what He actually said.

There are only a couple of people I have met who said that they actually heard the voice of the Lord out loud, and that was a one-time occurrence at a pivotal moment in their lives. Far be it from me to limit the Lord in how He speaks. Most people who listen for the Lord hear a quiet inner voice spoken by the Holy Spirit to their spirit, understood by their mind.

There have been a number of times when I have not been able to hear the Lord until I have come to the end of myself. Especially in times of stress or anxiety, I have been so full of my own rushing thoughts. When I spend time with Him, sometimes my thoughts are racing, full of my troubles. When I have poured them out to Him and come to the end of them, then I am finally able to listen to what He has to say. I am learning to come more quickly and spread everything out before Him so that I can listen more thoroughly. There is such great value in being still in His presence, and in expressing our love and praise to Him.

I am ashamed to admit that there have been times when I didn't want to obey Him, because I was uncomfortable with what He was asking me to do. Before my husband and I had children, I worked as an office manager for an import-export firm. The owner was often gone overseas arranging contracts with suppliers. He trusted me to keep the company running in his absence. We had a very good rapport and often talked about the meaning of life including faith. He loved classical music, literature, and art. When it was almost time to have our first child, I resigned my position.

Seven years later, I realized that the Holy Spirit was putting this man on my heart. Day after day it continued. I knew that I was supposed to contact him. The Spirit impressed upon me that I had never really explained to my former boss how to believe in Christ as his personal Savior, how to trust in Jesus. I was very uncomfortable about the idea of contacting him after not speaking to him for seven years! I argued that I wouldn't even know what to say! And how would I even know where he was? Two days later I went to a Bible study which had the topic of "What to Say to Someone Who Needs to Hear the Gospel." Okay, I was getting the message. I decided that I should sit down and write him a letter and let God handle how to get it there.

After a time of prayer, the Holy Spirit helped me as I sat down with pen and paper. The letter practically wrote itself with God's help and it made the plan of salvation clear, outlining Scripture which would be helpful for this man to read. Then I called up an old phone number I had for him. His wife answered the phone, and I found out that they had been divorced for several years. But she went on to say that he would no doubt enjoy hearing from me, so she gave me his address in another state. I prayed fervently as I put a stamp on the letter and mailed it. I had no idea how the letter would be received.

Two weeks later I got a phone call. It was my former boss. His first words to me were, "Why did you send me that letter?" I couldn't tell from his tone of voice whether he was upset, surprised, questioning, or receptive. I explained as best I could that he had repeatedly been put on my heart by God, and that I was to write and explain what God had provided for us in Christ. There was silence, and then in a warm tone of voice, he replied, "Your letter was a miracle of timing. I had always wanted to read the Bible as a classical piece of literature. I picked it up a few weeks ago and have not been able to stop reading it since. I have read enough to have a number of questions about Jesus, but I didn't know where to get answers. Then I got your letter."

We went on to have a lengthy conversation, and he told me that he was very close to trusting Christ as his Savior. A few weeks later he called me and told me that he had trusted in Christ, and he was going to be baptized. At Christmas time he sent me a card saying that Christmas had come alive for him in all new ways. Despite my initial reluctance to obey God's leading, for which I asked His forgiveness, I was so glad that the Lord persisted and made it possible for me to reach out to this man. The Lord could have used someone else, but I am so glad that I was able to witness firsthand the amazing love of God and His precise timing in bringing this special man to Himself.

It has been easier and easier to hear the Lord as I continue to learn from Him and walk with Him closely. I have shared in another chapter about my spiritual retreat in Wyoming on my way to a conference in Chicago. On one of my evenings in Chicago the Lord asked me to take a walk with Him. I walked down to Millennium Park crossing Michigan Avenue during a very busy rush hour. The Bandshell in the park was gearing up for a concert. I sat down almost hidden by a tree. The noise was tremendous. People were streaming into the concert venue, talking, and laughing excitedly. The vehicle traffic was very noisy on Michigan Avenue, and on the corner nearby a man had set up a set of drums. He seemed to want to impress everyone within earshot and kept up a steady stream of drumbeats.

In the midst of all of this sound, the Holy Spirit's voice spoke clearly to my spirit. "You are worried that you will not be able to hear Me as clearly as you did in the cabin in Wyoming. I want to show you that I am always with you. Even in the midst of all this sound, you can clearly hear what I want to say to you." I was very surprised. I had not fully realized how concerned I was about this very thing. How gracious of the Lord to show me this in such a graphic way that I could not forget it. It was the very next day when He sent me to talk to the woman I met at the conference.

God's thoughts are not my thoughts, for He says things which are unexpected. He reveals truth and His perspective which often includes specific guidance. He points things out I could not have known, and He is so very loving. Sometimes He gives me correction which I need, and He is always restorative, wanting me to walk closer to Him. There have been a handful of times when He has approached me with majesty and authority. Those times are unmistakable, and then I usually go to my knees, humbly listening carefully for His every word. Those have often been turning points in my life which He didn't want me to miss. He is the Lord, and He has all wisdom. When I listen to Him and obey Him, I am always blessed.

I have mentioned before that I have at times treated the Lord like a vending machine. I wanted to put in my prayers, hear guidance from Him, and run off to implement things according to my own plans. It becomes obvious quickly at those times that I am not walking with Him for I do not have any of His strength, peace, joy, or wisdom. I am not abiding in Him because I have left His side to do things myself.

There is one other area where I have had to learn some hard lessons. I have tried several times to treat the Lord as a fortune teller. I wanted to know the future so that I would know how to plan for it. Sometimes I wanted to know so that it could alleviate my anxiety. This became a real issue when my husband was first diagnosed with his condition and was told he didn't have long to live. I wanted the Lord to let me know the future. The Lord reminded me that He would be with me, and He told me to stop seeking to know the future. I have struggled in this area several times. When we don't obey the Lord, we will get into grievous errors. When He doesn't reply with what we want, we can fill in the blank with our own words or thoughts, and the enemy of our souls finds easy entry. And the truth is, if I were always told the future I would likely run off on my own and make my plans, without walking each step with the God who shares with us each moment. We don't find God in the past; the past is already gone. We can learn from the past and see evidence of His working, but we find Him right now, in the moment. Yes, He will also be with us in the future. But it is our moment by moment walk with Him which is the key to sharing our lives with Him.

As we walk each day with Him, we will be walking all of our tomorrows with Him as well. We do not have to be anxious about the future, for He will be there. I have to be careful not to run off without Him, or to want to know things which it is not wise for me to know yet. And the Lord has been so dear and near to me in the midst of suffering. He has come so close, been so gentle, so reassuring. He has brought truth, comfort, encouragement and even surprised me with joy. He has become my oasis in the midst of dark valleys. He has reminded me of His wonderful promises. In the midst of great storms of trial, pain, and grief He has held me tenderly and gently close to His heart. In the midst of His presence there is great stillness and His calm.

Lift everything to Him, spread it before Him. Seek His counsel. Place everything into His hands. KNOW that He is there. If you are willing to follow Him, He will lead, for He has promised to be our good shepherd. He made us for relationship and incredibly wants a personal walk with each one of us. He has done everything to make that possible. He delights in us and calls us His beloved. That is a level of intimacy which so few choose to take Him up on. He DELIGHTS in you. He wants you to come to Him. Invite Him into everything with you. He knows it all already.

Do you really want to walk alone? If you keep Him at a distance, you will not be abiding in Him, and His life will not flow through you. You will only have your own weakness, your own thoughts instead of His truths, your own pitiful comfort when you could have all that He has in store for you. Alone you will have such short-range eyesight instead of His eternal perspective. You will not have the power of His Spirit flowing through your life or working in and through you, and worst of all you will not know Him. You will not know how loving and beautiful it is to walk with Him. Walking with Him brings healing for past hurts and incredible freedom to be loved by Him and to be used in ways which have eternal significance.

If you knew that your Savior and Lord Jesus was in a certain place on earth and all you had to do to talk with Him or hear Him would be to travel where He was, would you? He is right here, right now. He is near to all of us who call upon Him in truth. That is one of the reasons the Holy Spirit was given to us, to make us alive to God.

John 16:7 "But I tell you the truth, it is to your advantage that I go away; for if I do not go away, the Helper will not come to you; but if I go, I will send Him to you."

John 16:13 "But when He, the Spirit of truth, comes, He will guide you into all the truth; for He will not speak on His own initiative, but whatever He hears, He will speak."

God does not desire to stand afar off, to be a stranger to us. He put a new covenant in place so that He could have a new heart relationship with us. Oh, turn and seek Him. He is nearer to you than you can imagine.

Acts 17:27 "That they would seek God, if perhaps they might grope for Him and find Him, though He is not far from each one of us."

Psalm 63:1 "O God, You are my God; I shall seek You earnestly; my soul thirsts for You, my flesh yearns for You, in a dry and weary land where there is no water."

Come, walk with the One who freely gives living water and rest for your soul. The greatest adventure in life is waiting for you. The journey to walk and talk with the

Eternal One begins with just one step, and then the next. He wants you to share your heart with Him and to invite Him to walk with you, great treasure awaits.

CHAPTER 7

COURAGE

Psalm 27:14 "Wait for the LORD; be strong and let your heart take courage; yes, wait for the LORD."

In the Scriptures, God exhorted His people a number of times to take courage. His people encountered daunting challenges and overwhelming circumstances, and in their helplessness, they needed to stand and take courage. Did they have enough in themselves to meet the challenge? No they didn't, but they were told to be strong in the Lord. As Psalm 27:14 reminds us, "Wait for the Lord." He is the One in whom we have confidence.

When my children were little, my husband ran a business out of our home. I was the bookkeeper. We had several employees and were staying fairly busy. A virus spread throughout the community which was causing people to experience extreme vertigo. John came down with the virus and was ill for a few weeks, unable to work. For a few people, the virus did permanent damage to the inner ear. My husband's balance system in his right ear was wiped out, permanently. It was like a radio that only gives off static. It was sending erratic signals which prevented his left side from functioning properly. He could not walk, and even when he tried to crawl, he would fall over. They gave John some medication which helped a little. Then they told him he needed cranial surgery to sever the nerve leading to his right balance system so that he could learn to walk using his left side only. With great courage he accepted this diagnosis and went forward with the surgery.

The challenges were mounting. John fought hard to regain the ability to walk again using the balance system on his left side in combination with his vision. In the meantime, our employees were supposed to be working to keep things going in the business. Instead, they took advantage of the situation. They did a very poor job for several of our customers, and we were informed they were using drugs on another job site. This cost us most of our job contracts, and we were unable to meet our company's financial obligations. John's health was improving, but I knew that our company was not going to make it. I didn't know how we were going to provide for our family. At that point I was involved in a Bible study which focused on Habakkuk. The prophet knew that his country was going to be devastated.

In Habakkuk Chapter 3:16-19 it says:
"I must wait quietly for the day of distress…"
"Though the fig tree should not blossom and there be no fruit on the vines, though the yield of the olive should fail and the fields produce no food, though the flock should be cut off from the fold and there be no cattle in the stalls, yet I will exult in the LORD, I will rejoice in the God of my salvation. The Lord GOD is my strength, and He has made my feet like hinds' feet, and makes me walk on my high places."

I really related to these verses. I knew that we were financially in distress, but with the help of these verses I decided to take courage and trust in God. I couldn't see how He would provide, but I determined to rejoice in God and wait and watch for His deliverance. When the leader of the Bible study asked what we had learned that year, I said that I had learned a lot more about faith in the midst of trials. I commented that my trust in God was still a work in progress, but that if the Lord were to leave me in trials, I was sure that my trust in Him would grow. I could not have foreseen how prophetic those words would be.

Even though I was determined to trust, it wasn't easy. We sold everything that we had of any value. We lived with family for a time, and experienced God's provision in surprising ways. We moved several times over the next four years and eventually settled near Dallas, Texas where John obtained a job with a company which provided high level training and launched him into a new career. We still had a substantial unresolved debt with the IRS for our former business. It looked like we would be paying on that for the rest of our lives, especially as interest would no doubt be added.

During this same time, I had been dealing with a lot of pain in my abdomen. They couldn't seem to find the problem. After we moved to the Dallas area and had been able to get some health insurance, I sought out a physician. He dismissed my concerns and told me it was all psychological. This was extremely discouraging and was no help to me at all. After all the moves and changes in our lives and with the physical pain I was enduring, I was at a real low point. I kept trying to pray but I felt that my prayers were not reaching past the ceiling. I felt like I was in a wilderness, especially since we knew no one in the area and had not found a church home yet. I finally retreated to my bedroom and took the time to start writing notes about what I was feeling and thinking: discouragement, distress, anxiety, doubt, pain. It was overwhelming. At the bottom of the list, I stopped. I had a choice. I wrote in big letters, I BELIEVE GOD.

I chose not to rely on my feelings or my fears. I needed to take courage and put all of my trust in God. Little by little He led me out of the darkness of discouragement. I made the choice to begin to praise, not because I felt like it, but because it was right and true. I realized later that when we are in the wilderness, we are in good company with people like Moses, David, Paul, and even Jesus Himself. They all had wilderness experiences. The Lord knew our future, and He knew how many years of trial we were going to go through. I needed to learn this lesson so that no matter what the circumstances were or how I was feeling, the foundation stone of my life would be centered on believing God. This held me securely in the midst of the storms which were to follow.

A few months later I found a wonderful physician who correctly identified my physical pain which was totally relieved with surgery. After praying earnestly about the tax situation, the Lord granted us favor with the IRS. I worked with an IRS agent who provided an "offer in compromise" which allowed us to pay off our debt to the IRS with the earnings from the new job. In time John found great success at his new job, and he was offered a higher-level position by a manufacturer who moved us to the West Coast.

The Lord knew that we would soon be involved with a 25-year journey which would involve suffering, huge challenges, and yet great blessings as well. God also knew that we would need the help of a certain neurosurgeon on the West Coast close to our home who had great experience in exactly the rare condition which my husband was battling. We could not have walked through those years without the Lord as our foundation and our strength.

He was teaching us to have courage and faith. His is the power that overcomes.

John 16:33 (Jesus said) "These things I have spoken to you, so that in Me you may have peace. In the world you have tribulation, but take courage, I have overcome the world."

Most people I know have a default setting when they face challenges or are confronted with trouble. Most of them default to either fear or anger. Those things by themselves are not a problem, but what we do with them is extremely important. If we choose to dwell in them, then we can act in unwise ways which can have devastating consequences. I have always battled with fear. I have become very familiar with three main types of fear in my life.

There is healthy fear which hopefully we learn as we grow and mature. That is the kind of fear which makes you not run into traffic or put your hand in a fire. It keeps you safe. There is a healthy fear of God in which we acknowledge that He is the Sovereign One, and we are not. He is due all praise and worship. He is the creator, and we are His creation. We should have great awe when we contemplate who He is, and a reverence for what He says and a desire to obey Him. He is able to save us.

Psalm 33:8 "Let all the earth fear the Lord, let all the inhabitants of the world stand in awe of Him."

Psalm 33:18 "Behold, the eye of the Lord is on those who fear Him, on those who hope for His lovingkindness."

Proverbs 14:26 "In the fear of the Lord there is strong confidence, and His children will have refuge."

I have experienced fear and anxiety which is not healthy. I have explained in earlier chapters about my previous habit of worrying and being anxious about so many things. This kind of fear is almost crippling at times. It prevents us from really living in the present in healthy ways or enjoying the freedom to walk in peace and joy. Instead, our minds are filled up with so much fear and a variety of "what ifs." The sad part is that we can't really change much by worrying about it. We don't know the future, and many of the fears we spend so much energy on never come to pass at all. Worrying about them actually creates so much stress that it affects our physical, mental, and emotional wellbeing. It also affects our spiritual walk, because we spend so much time on fear that we are not very useful in carrying out the purposes of God which we should be about. And we are certainly not trusting Him when we are holding on so tightly to fear. Our vision becomes clouded, and our ears are not usually listening to Him.

Let us pray, "Oh Lord, give us the courage to let go of anxiety and fear, and grasp instead your wonderful promises. Fill our minds with who You are, the faithful One who never leaves us or forsakes us. Help us to have the courage to bring all that we are concerned about and entrust it to You."

There is another type of fear which I have battled. This fear is wielded by the enemy of our souls. Even though I cannot fully see the spiritual battle around me, the Scriptures tell us about it in Ephesians 6:10-18. The Lord tells us repeatedly in these verses to be strong and to stand firm. This takes courage when we are in the midst of a battle. We must have the truth of God's Word and the shield of faith which is "able to extinguish all the flaming arrows of the evil one."

Many times in my life I have experienced fear which I believe to be a flaming arrow from the evil one. My enemy knows this is a weakness of mine which he just might get me to pay attention to. When I turn to God and trust in Him, I ask Him to remove this unreasoning fear and take it far from me. Many times there is immediate relief, and the fear is gone.

Doubt is another matter. If I listen to the lies of the enemy even for a few seconds, if I give way to fear, it starts sowing seeds of doubt. The shield of faith, my choice to trust in God, can protect me and keep the enemy from having an influence on my mind, heart, and spirit. But if even momentarily I start to entertain these fears and listen to thoughts which question the truth or the goodness of God, I have let the enemy inside my defenses. All too quickly doubt takes root.

A couple of years ago I was on a spiritual retreat with the Lord. He was showing me many things from His Word and the time was very sweet and special. On the last night I awoke in the middle of the night and found myself experiencing fear which was ramping up quickly. Then thoughts came which launched doubts about the truth I had just been learning. I am ashamed to say that I listened to them and started to entertain some doubts about what I had just been hearing from the Lord. The Holy Spirit helped me to realize this was an attack from the enemy. I asked the Lord to remove the fear, and it was instantly gone. I asked for His forgiveness for entertaining the doubts and asked Him to remove all doubt. His answer surprised me. He said that He wouldn't remove the doubt from me. I needed to do the work of countering the doubts with the truth.

I immediately reviewed all of the truth which the Lord had been showing me, and I read again all of the Scripture which He had been sharing with me. It effectively removed all doubt and replaced it with the bedrock of His truth. I still felt ashamed that I had listened and participated in the furtherance of doubtful thoughts, but the Lord quickly forgave and restored me right back to His side. He knows our weaknesses. He knows we are not strong enough in ourselves, but we can take courage, come back to Him, and with His help stand firm. We can be strong in Him.

I wrote the lines below which have often come back to me when things are challenging, or I am tempted to fear. When my emotions are clamoring, I can take courage and by a choice of my will choose to trust and praise.

Fear and doubt are like thieves in the night
Trying to break in and steal,
Robbing our joy and overwhelming our sight
Until nothing around us seems real.
Name them then, recognize the foe
And then to God's promises cling.
Don't let those thieves deprive you of joy,
Instead let His praises ring.

Let me say just a few words about spiritual battles. There are times when we are overwhelmed or weak in the midst of the battle. Sometimes we are just tired because it has been a long haul. First, try to make sure you are getting enough rest because when we are very tired, we are easy prey. Second, try to seek out God's truth and promises and trust Him. Third, it may be time for a spiritual 911. When you are too weak to stand firm, ask others to spiritually stand with you in the battle or to help hold you up when you cannot stand. Ask them to pray for you, to bring you to the throne of grace with them.

Hebrews 4:16 "Therefore let us draw near with confidence to the throne of grace, so that we may receive mercy and find grace to help in time of need."

Remember also that our Lord Jesus is our Savior, and He is interceding for us.

Hebrews 7:25 "Therefore He is able also to save forever those who draw near to God through Him, since He always lives to make intercession for them."

Be part of the prayer response team for others who are unable to stand firm in their battle. The enemy of our souls is constantly trying to confuse us with half-truths. He loves to accuse us and draw us away from our standing in Christ. Bring yourself and others to the foot of the cross. Remember that Jesus won the victory by His sacrifice on the cross. He defeated the enemy there. You are His, so stand in the victory that He won on our behalf. Since we are God's beloved children, tell the enemy that he must take his accusations or attacks or lies into the very presence of God, who is your Father. God can silence the enemy. The Holy Spirit will remind you of truth and help you to stand fast knowing that you are loved by your Father in heaven. You are forgiven and free to walk with God in a close and intimate relationship.

There is another type of courage I want to mention. It is the courage to do things differently than the world, with integrity and grace. Many of us have jobs which are very busy. Sometimes people urge us to cut corners for the sake of expediency, but God is always interested in our honest work efforts. We usually have many things to get done. Our minds can be so full of our daily activities that we don't take time to lift our eyes to the things above. I was a very busy manager, with my division personnel scattered over seven buildings. As I walked between buildings to go meet with people and tackle my list of things to do, my mind was usually occupied with the latest challenge or problem to solve. I was so engrossed with it I didn't even lift my eyes to see the blue sky overhead or the beautiful shade trees I was walking under.

There is a quiet courage that we need to develop. It is the courage to stop and seek the things above, gain God's perspective, and choose to abide in Him. Of all the people on earth, Christians should be the most joyful. We have been forgiven, set free, promised an eternal inheritance and a place with Him, and we have the wonderful privilege of walking with Him daily. As we abide in Him, His Spirit overflows with joy. But if we are honest, we must admit that often we appear much like the rest of the world. We are so burdened with our stuff, trying to solve our problems on our own, that we end up leaving Him out. Then we are not abiding. I decided to put a stop sign on the back of my office door. I wrote the initials IHO on the stop sign. I wanted to remind myself that in any situation I needed to stop and remember that "It's His Opportunity."

Problems are not always easy to solve, but many times I realized it was an opportunity to show His grace, and I needed His wisdom. It helped to transform my days. I started lifting everything in my day to Him. I was surprised at how He would clarify my priorities for the day and give me clear thinking about what I needed to prepare ahead of time. He gave me wisdom to handle tough situations and to find solutions for things which had been in disarray long before I got there. And even more importantly, He helped me to do it by building bridges to people and developing collaborative relationships with them.

When we are abiding with Him, our workdays should look different from those that don't know Him. We should have a calm purpose, and a joyful attitude, for He brings good. He has things He wants us to be involved in. As I walked with Him through my days, I started looking up, listening for His guidance, and I began noticing the sky, the trees, and even more importantly really seeing the people in front of me.

My default setting in the midst of trouble is fear, but for some it is anger. I have lived with and around others who struggle with anger which can quickly reach the boiling point. It is not easy to overcome. There are many things in this world which try our patience, and which are sometimes completely unfair or unnecessary. We can often feel helpless especially during times of pain, or when we face limitations or when those we love are suffering.

At other times people do things which are careless or even intentionally harmful. Feelings of anger surface quickly and thoughts of retribution dance through our minds. This can consume us almost completely in the moment. Anger can be very blinding, and when we give way to expressing it, we often don't realize or sometimes don't even care that we are hurting others. When the anger subsides, we sometimes try to repair the damage done to those around us who were unintended victims of our outrage. In some cases, the damage can even be intentional since in our anger we were trying to make others bend to our will or at least agree with us.

When we act in anger it can cause a lot of harm to others around us, and it can also cause negative effects for us on the inside both physically and emotionally, especially the longer we hold on to it. Scripture exhorts us to not dwell in it or harbor it.

Ephesians 4:26 "Be angry, and yet do not sin; do not let the sun go down on your anger."

Is there hope to get a grip on our anger? Anger in itself is a normal enough reaction but how we choose to handle it, whether we choose to embrace it and to simmer in it or turn from it is the key. There is hope, but it will take courage. It will take the courage to face it, STOP, and not excuse ourselves when we hurt others with it.

Anger is almost always a secondary emotion triggered by pain, frustration, injustice, fear, inconvenience, or other causes. In our quieter moments, we realize there are better ways to deal with the situation. We must realize that anger can have devastating effects especially on our families and other close relationships. They are often the ones most impacted since they are close to us when anger flares into outbursts.

You need to find a healthy way to express your anger. Give yourself permission to acknowledge when you are angry. Try to identify the cause, which may lead toward understanding. Do not give yourself permission to spew your anger toward the closest person with whom you come in contact. Do you value your relationships? Acting in anger can drive them away quickly, or at the very least make them wary of being near you. And if the closest person to you usually defaults to fear, guess what will happen when you display your anger? They will become fearful! We are always either building up our relationships or tearing them down. In order to find help with anger, why not take it to God? He knows it anyway. He is big enough to handle it and can help you if you will let Him.

When you experience anger, try to stop and recognize the truth in the situation, be honest about it. Surrender it to the Lord. He has said that vengeance is His. Do you believe Him? Can you trust Him with it, or do you insist on running off to take care of things on your own? I have seen great injustices at high levels in the workplace. Other people's actions were impacting me and many of the people that I worked with. I prayed for justice, because the Lord knows the hearts and the truth about the situations more than I do. In the two most appalling cases, the Lord totally removed the people from their positions and brought justice, order, and peace. Praise be to God! Can you have the courage to wait for the Lord and for His deliverance?

Be humble and honest with others and ask for their forgiveness if they have borne the brunt of your anger. If you are serious about changing how you deal with anger, don't excuse it. Always go to anyone you have wronged and try to repair the relationship. Don't try to justify your angry actions because of what you were angry about, instead make amends for the damage you have inflicted. Own your part.

Value others more than you value your anger. It is more important for us to love those around us than to stand on our soapboxes and hold on to our right to vent our anger. If necessary, find a safe place to express your anger and then relinquish it. Trust the Lord to right the wrongs and fight your battles even if it takes longer than you want it to. In humility turn to Him and ask for His strength to give you the courage you need.

I have spoken in other chapters about receiving God's help to heal the pain of the past, especially those things that have hurt us and which we have carried for a long time. It takes courage to relinquish things which we hold so close to ourselves. It takes courage to find a new way, to walk into the freedom and the life which God wants to give us. Ask Him for the strength to take the first steps. Take courage and trust that as He leads you, He will also heal and bless. He will be with you, as you open up your entire life and heart to Him.

We live in a world of people who all have needs. Often people want so many things, and they go about getting them in all the wrong ways. When people hurt us, it takes courage for us to choose to forgive. Notice that I didn't say to feel like forgiving. It will never depend on our feelings. Like everything else in the Christian life, our real transactions with God and with ourselves will depend on our will, on our choices. God takes us at our word. Let us take Him at His word. He has asked us to forgive. Haven't we been forgiven much ourselves? Sin cost our dear Savior his very life. He endured great suffering and still uttered the words, "Father forgive them." He can give us the courage to forgive others. This is not a trifling matter or empty words. I was severely abused by someone whom I loved and who was supposed to love me. I had a choice. Here again I hear the Savior's words, "Do you want to be well?" Love or forgiveness do not depend on whether the person deserves it or not. It is a choice on our part, and I chose to forgive with God's help.

Relinquish the hurt to God, let Him help you to forgive those who have wronged you. Put them into the hands of God. You will find healing for your soul. This does not mean that you need to put yourself into a trust relationship with that person again. They may not be trustworthy. It may not be possible to have a close relationship with them unless they are willing to repent and fundamentally change with the help of God. But you no longer have to harbor bitterness, anger, or resentment. Let it go. Walk freely with the Lord remembering how much He has forgiven you. And if you have hurt someone else, be courageous and go ask for their forgiveness. It is part of the process which heals and restores.

I am very acquainted with suffering, sorrow, and grief. When our loved one dies and is a believer, we have the sure hope that they are with the Lord. They are safe, joyful, healthy, and very much alive in a far better place. But our grief and loss is very real. The departure of the person we loved has left a hole in our lives which cannot be filled.

It is a normal part of loving someone to grieve for them after they are gone. Even though there has been much written about the stages of grief, they come at different times and in a different order than we expect. And just when we think we are starting to adjust, we are surprised and revisited with grief which can be triggered by a memory, or a date on the calendar, or a reminder of our loss once again. Grief is so bittersweet.

Sometimes we don't want to turn from grief because it seems that our grief helps us to hold our loved one closer to us. We cling to the loss and are tempted to give way to overwhelming sadness and a dark pit of despair. I would gently ask you to bring that to your Father God. He understands sorrow and death, and hates what it does to His creation. He sent Jesus to defeat death so it would no longer be the final word. He will help you relinquish your loved one to Him and turn from the deep despairing grief that is overwhelming.

Stand on your feet, take courage, and ask Him to take your hand and lead you out of the darkness into the light. By relinquishing your loved one to the Lord you will not lose their memory or their closeness. Quite the contrary, you will be enabled to see more clearly the treasures they deposited into your life that no one can take away from you. Hold onto those things in the light and with the help of God. He longs to wipe away your tears. God's love soothes and comforts. He reminds us of His eternal truth and His promises. He carries us when we are unable to stand, and He is patient and gentle with us.

The grieving process can certainly take a while, and you will always miss your loved one, but the Lord wants you to stand up and walk on, back into life. He still has a purpose for you during your time on earth. If your loved one took care of many things and you are not certain how to manage them, seek out wise counselors, experts, brothers and sisters in Christ or friends who can help you put things in place which you will need in order to carry on. Take courage. You are not alone.

When we lose someone, or when our world changes, sometimes we seem to lose our identity. This has happened to me several times in my life. It can happen when relationships change or are lost, when our job changes, when we move to a new place, or when we change churches or ministries. The one constant thing about life is that there will be changes!! We need the courage to keep our identity focused on Christ.

When our identity is rooted in anything else, it will shift fundamentally when things change. Often we work on creating our own identity and then compare ourselves to others around us. Depending on who we compare ourselves to will depend on whether we feel good about ourselves or not. This is building an identity on shifting sand.

Take courage and seek your identity in Christ. God's love for us does not waver or fluctuate. He counts us of infinite worth, after all Christ died to save you. He wants to walk with you. He has a purpose for your life which is unique to you. You are special to Him, beloved. Don't rely upon other things to give you worth, they will not always be there for you. God is unchangeable. His love never fails for He is the faithful One. Come and enjoy His love and walk with Him heart to heart.

If we want to walk closely with God, we will need the courage to confront sin. If you are a believer, you have the Holy Spirit living within you. It is incredible that the HOLY Spirit lives within the hearts of unholy people, but we have been covered with the righteousness of Christ. We have become alive to God.

We will not have the freedom and joy to walk fully with God if we harbor sin in our life. Don't cozy up to it or excuse it. Have the courage to confront it and call it for what it is. I want to say something radical here. We do not have to walk in sin. We are no longer slaves to sin. If we walk in fellowship with the Almighty, by the help of His Holy Spirit, we do not have to sin. The enemy may send disturbing thoughts into our minds, but those are not sin unless we harbor them or agree with them and act on them. We can identify these transitory unhealthy thoughts and give them to God to dispose of and walk on undisturbed in our fellowship.

Sometimes we do things we didn't realize were wrong, and the Holy Spirit points it out and helps us to have the courage to learn from it and correct our actions. I have not always obeyed the Lord immediately, and I have needed to ask for His forgiveness and then move to obey. Confronting our sin will take extreme honesty and transparency and humility. Part of the work of the Holy Spirit is to convict us of sin. We must agree with Him when He points it out, confess and receive His forgiveness and restoration. If we have sinned against others, we sometimes need to have the courage to ask for their forgiveness and seek restoration or make restitution where needed.

Romans 12:18 "If possible, so far as it depends on you, be at peace with all men."

It takes work, courage, and prayer to mend relationships. When we do those things, it helps us to learn to treat people differently in the first place. It helps our speech to be more gracious, and our prayers for others to be more loving. It gives us the desire to live at peace with others and seek restoration in relationships. The Scripture does say "so far as it depends on you." There are times when the person you are approaching is difficult and is holding on to anger or bitterness toward you and will not forgive. Pray for them. They may not see it, but this is a heavy burden they are carrying around. Pray for the Lord to change their hearts, which is a work only He can do when they are willing. It is so much more freeing to walk in peace.

As I have walked with the Lord, He has often called me into new positions, new ministries, new places. You would think that I would be used to that by now, but the truth is that change is difficult for all of us. The Lord is able to give us the courage to walk in new ways, taking new steps with hope. In Acts 13:36 it says that David served the purposes of God in his generation. God challenges us to love and care about others and to invest in helping them come to know and love God.

Let us not be content to sit on the sidelines, no matter our age or place in life. Even if we have poor health, we can reach out to others in many ways, and we can be praying for them. Prayer accomplishes more than we know. Invite the Lord to work in their lives, entrust them to Him.

Have the courage to serve the purposes of God in your generation. God's arm is not short. He is looking for those whose heart is completely His. Great is His power toward those who believe. Take courage, be strong in the Lord and in the strength of His might. He will ultimately overcome.

CHAPTER 8

SACRIFICE

We often honor those who risk their lives for others, and when they pay the ultimate price, we are humbled by their sacrifice. I was traveling with my family visiting Washington, D.C. Near the monument honoring our veterans of the Korean War there was a sign that read, "Freedom is Not Free." It was a sobering reminder of how much has been sacrificed by our military personnel on behalf of our country.

I was able to visit a museum in Boston a few years ago. On exhibit they had an early version of the Declaration of Independence which had notes from its authors on what words they wanted to change or add. I couldn't help thinking about those who had signed the final document and who risked everything, especially if they were caught during the Revolutionary War. I appreciate their commitment and their willing sacrifice in the cause of something much bigger than themselves.

The firefighters on 9/11 did not think twice. They ran into the Twin Towers in New York in order to save as many as they could. The men on Flight 93 likewise sacrificed everything to try to save everyone on the flight as well as avoid further casualties if the plane were crashed into its intended target. We continue to honor their sacrifices.

There are other types of sacrifice. My parents were missionaries to remote areas of South America. They left families and loved ones behind not knowing when they would see them again. This was before computers or cell phones. Phone service was unreliable and phone calls were terribly expensive. They relied on letters from home to stay connected, even though the postal service was sometimes not very efficient. I remember that when my grandfather died, we didn't hear about it until much later. My parents left their culture and country behind because God asked them to go. They developed a deep love for the people where they went, and they used every opportunity to tell them about the love of God.

Eventually my parents returned and pastored churches in the United States. Despite a large family and a small salary, my Dad was a careful steward of what he was given, and the Lord provided. My Dad knew that he needed to be responsible to save some funds toward retirement because he didn't want to be a burden on others. He was somehow able to save faithfully. He retired first in his late sixties, but then was immediately called to go serve as a bilingual pastor in a church in Arizona near the border with Mexico. He faithfully followed God's leadership. After a few years there, he retired again.

My Mom and Dad drove up to Phoenix to arrange for the start of distribution payments to be made to fund their retirement. The doors had just been locked to the building. The person in charge of the foundation had created shell corporations and taken the money. The funds could not be found, and no one knew if any of the money would be recovered.

My parents came to stay in our home for a while. We had planned to travel to go see a family member. In order to save money, we all stayed in the same hotel room together. Just before going to bed, my parents received a phone call saying that it looked like all of their retirement money was gone. At around 2:00 a.m. I woke up and heard my parents talking. My Dad was apologizing to my Mom. He said, "I am so sorry. I thought that I had planned for our retirement so that you would never be in need." My Mom's immediate reply was, "We have trusted in God all of our lives. We are not about to stop trusting now." Dad went on to pastor another church. The church had a parsonage, so my parents were able to save quite a bit of their salary. Some of their retirement funds were surprisingly recovered within a few years, and by the time Dad retired for the third time, he had enough money to buy a little place near us. He continued to serve in his local church as a Pastor to seniors, preaching and working with a nursing home ministry, and serving as a hospital chaplain until he passed away. My parents were a wonderful example of sacrificing their lives for the sake of investing in other people.

I have witnessed and experienced a number of situations where people who are enduring suffering offer a sacrifice of praise. I have written about the rare condition which my husband had which caused bleeding in the brain. We spent a lot of time in emergency rooms, intensive care units and medical offices, and we participated in experimental treatments. My husband had a lot of pain and suffering, and there was great uncertainty about how long he would live. Many things were out of our control, but we had control over our responses. We could choose what we focused on and where to put our trust. And the Lord taught us to "sing in the night," so we offered our sacrifices of praise. God is good, and He brought blessings time after time.

Ten years after my husband's diagnosis, our son was driving to high school and had a car accident. It quickly became apparent that the accident was caused by something serious. An MRI revealed that our son had the same condition as his Dad. We didn't know until then that it was genetic. Our son needed brain surgery. I was in tears thinking of what this meant for his life, but I entrusted him to the Lord. His brain bleed was very close to the part of the brain which deals with speech. They said that the surgery might affect his ability to speak. You can imagine my relief when I walked into the recovery room, and he said clearly, "Hi, Mom!" Some of his words were jumbled for a few weeks, but he recovered fully. Two years later he had an even riskier surgery on his spinal cord. The surgeon was concerned about possible paralysis. I entrusted my son again into the hands of God. I felt a little of what Abraham must have felt when he was asked to sacrifice his precious son, and he chose to trust in God's plan. The surgeon was able to operate, and the problem area was more accessible than they had dared hope. It took courage and resilience, but in time our son recovered.

One of our daughters was on a ministry team with a Christian music group. An MRI showed that she had the same brain condition as her Dad and her brother, affecting a number of areas in her brain. Within a year she needed to have her first brain surgery. I won't go into all of the details because these are my children's stories to tell. I would gladly have taken their conditions and symptoms upon myself if I could have spared them. These were difficult times, but we were never alone.

Our daughter had learned several years before about the sacrifice of praise. At the time she was a teenager who was part of the worship team of our church. She started having debilitating back spasms which we prayed about. One Sunday morning she just couldn't physically get up and go to church. I prayed for her and sat beside her as she tearfully asked why the Lord wouldn't remove this from her? All she wanted to do was be a part of worshipping Him that morning. I gently asked her a question. Which would honor the Lord more? Would it honor Him more for her to be part of the worship team that morning, or for her to offer a sacrifice of praise and worship Him from her bed? Despite her pain, she chose to start praising. It was a blessed time that she and I never forgot.

It says in Psalm 32:7, "You are my hiding place; You preserve me from trouble; You surround me with songs of deliverance."

Some people have told me that I have strong faith. I can absolutely tell you that I do not. I have a little faith, but I have a STRONG GOD!! Through all of the trials I have been through, I have learned how weak I truly am. I do not have enough of anything, but the Lord has plenty. I can run to Him. Despite how little faith we have, what matters is who we place our faith in. I put my trust in the Lord who shares His strength, wisdom, peace, and love with me. With His help I have received what I need day by day. Praise His name!

We all struggle with suffering. There is plenty of it in this life. Sometimes people wonder why God doesn't alleviate all of it. I grew up in third world countries, in a culture which accepted suffering as a part of our daily lives. In affluent countries people seem to forget that suffering is a normal part of the era that we currently live in. As a result of sin, disease and death entered this world and that inevitably brings suffering. And then there is the suffering we endure from our own sin or the sin of others. I mentioned before that for a few years we became a shelter home for runaways for our county. Later we adopted two girls to provide them with a home and a future and give them hope. We saw so much evidence of broken homes and dysfunctional families.

Sin causes devastation. If the Lord were going to remove suffering, He would have to remove all of us from the planet, for we are all sinful. The only real way not to have suffering is to go live with Him where every tear is wiped away. But in order to get there, we would have to go through the process of decay and death!

Can Jesus heal? Of course, He can. There have been several occasions when as a direct answer to prayer my husband received sweet relief from his overwhelming symptoms for a period of time. And I am convinced that God honored John's prayers to live long enough to see his children grow up, despite the prognosis of his doctors. We were told by well-meaning people that if our faith were strong enough, he would be fully healed. Let me just say that this is a presumptuous statement. If the person who is suffering is not healed, then they either doubt their faith or they doubt God. In either case the last thing they need is to deal with doubt in the midst of their suffering.

God's Word instructs us to pray for healing, but God is the sovereign One. He decides on how He will answer. As difficult as it is for us to accept, His purposes are sometimes better served through the trial than if we were relieved of the trial. Shadrach, Meshach, and Abednego entrusted themselves completely to the Lord. They were not saved from the furnace; the Lord was their refuge as they went through the furnace. In the Bible it is clear that Paul had plenty of faith in the power of God. God performed healing works through him. And yet God did not heal him of his condition, instead God said that His grace would be sufficient for Paul. And Paul recognized that in his weakness, God could be glorified.

When Jesus was on earth, He did not heal everyone. Of those that He did heal, are they still alive today? Of course not, they died long ago. The physical healing that Jesus performed gave them health and extended their lives for a limited time only. Their healing was a sign of a much greater healing which they actually needed more. They needed spiritual life which would last for eternity. Their physical healing became evidence of God's ability to save forever. They were an awesome display of God's compassion and His purpose to rescue us.

I have seen the Lord heal people miraculously at times, but I have seen much greater miracles than physical healing. God is able to overcome bitterness and broken hearts. He is able to fill lives with love, grace and hope which had once been dark, shattered, empty, and lost. He does the miraculous work of putting His Holy Spirit within us. He takes us out of the darkness and into the light, and He makes us His beloved children. He changes us in deep and transformative ways. And He even gives us the privilege of being part of His plan to tell others about Christ so that they can pass from death into life everlasting.

We ask all of the wrong questions sometimes. Instead of second-guessing God's decisions, it would be better to ask why God loves us at all? Why would a Holy God choose to sacrifice His own Son to redeem unholy people? Why would the Lord of creation choose to empty Himself and be born as a man and humble Himself to the point of death? Why did our innocent Savior and glorious Lord choose to not save Himself, but instead allow Himself to be tortured and beaten, to be treated as a criminal and then ask His Father to forgive the people who put Him there?

2 Corinthians 8:9 tells us, "For you know the grace of our Lord Jesus Christ; that though He was rich, yet for your sake He became poor, that you through His poverty might become rich."

Jesus gave the ultimate sacrifice at great cost to Himself. The freedom which we now have in Christ was certainly not free. It cost Jesus dearly. We were dead spiritually because of our sin, but He sacrificed Himself so that the righteousness of Christ could become our covering for sin. By His wounds we are healed, and our sins are forgiven. He accomplished an amazing work through his death and resurrection. He made it possible for us to be born again and become God's children. We have an eternal inheritance with Him. We are given new spiritual life, and the Holy Spirit makes us alive to God.

Romans 6:10-11 "For the death that He died, He died to sin once for all, but the life that He lives, He lives to God. Even so consider yourselves to be dead to sin, but alive to God in Christ Jesus."

God raised Jesus from the dead. He conquered death for all of us. He is a Living God, and when we trust in Him, He shares His eternal life with us. We are alive to God in an eternal relationship that begins now and extends into eternity. It cost Him everything, and we must honor His great sacrifice by living as those who are now alive to Him. He did not sacrifice everything just so that we could experience forgiveness and then go off and live life on our own. Incredibly, He desires a close and intimate relationship with us which is amazingly tender and beautiful.

Philippians 2:5-11 "Have this attitude in yourselves which was also in Christ Jesus, who although He existed in the form of God, did not regard equality with God a thing to be grasped, but emptied Himself, taking the form of a bond-servant, and being made in the likeness of men. Being found in appearance as a man, He humbled Himself by becoming obedient to the point of death, even death on a cross. For this reason also, God highly exalted Him, and bestowed on Him the name which is above every name, so that at the name of Jesus every knee will bow, of those who are in heaven and on earth and under the earth, and that every tongue will confess that Jesus Christ is Lord, to the glory of God the Father."

Jesus released His grasp for a time on having the form of God so that he could become a man and sacrificially die for us. What are we grasping? What do we need to let go of? What needs to be sacrificed in order for us to walk with Him more closely so that He can be seen in our lives more clearly?

Galatians 2:20 "I have been crucified with Christ; and it is no longer I who live, but Christ lives in me, and the life which I now live in the flesh I live by faith in the Son of God, who loved me and delivered Himself up for me."

We must desire the Lord more than all else. Like our crucified Christ, we must trust God with all that we are and have confidence in His plan which is much better than ours. Respond to the Holy Spirit in willing surrender moment by moment. Respond to the Son who is our Good Shepherd, and follow Him, let Him lead you. Respond to the Father, worship Him, and let Him love you. Love the Lord your God.

The Lord will walk with you, be your guide, love you, restore you, heal your hurts, and be your strength in your weakness. We give Him all the glory, and He gives us Himself. There is no greater treasure on earth.

Take joy in His presence, abide, dwell in His wondrous grace and His love and peace. He is the living water, and these things flow from Him and do not run dry. Skip, sing and rejoice, for He is with us. The light of love shines in His eyes, and He pours life into our souls. Run with glad abandon to enjoy the heights with Him. Walk with compassion through the valleys, and with His help share His love with others. Many are lost and weary. We can tell them where to find rest for their souls.

Oh, I urge you. Take full advantage of your birthright as a child of God. He saved us in order to have an intimate relationship with us. Embrace the fact that you are alive to God. Don't allow anything to come between you and your Lord. Follow Him with gladness as His child who has complete trust in Him. Live life abundantly as you walk with Him step by step in utter dependence and joy.

1 Peter 1:3-8 "Blessed be the God and Father of our Lord Jesus Christ, who according to His great mercy has caused us to be born again to a living hope through the resurrection of Jesus Christ from the dead, to obtain an inheritance which is imperishable and undefiled and will not fade away, reserved in heaven for you, who are protected by the power of God through faith for a salvation ready to be revealed in the last time. In this you greatly rejoice, even though now for a little while, if necessary, you have been distressed by various trials, so that the proof of your faith, being more precious than gold which is perishable, even though tested by fire, may be found to result in praise and glory and honor at the revelation of Jesus Christ; and though you have not seen Him, you love Him, and though you do not see Him now, but believe in Him, you greatly rejoice with joy inexpressible and full of glory."

EPILOGUE

I have shared in these chapters about the illness of my husband, John. I talked about how the Lord led me to sell my house recently, retire early from my job and move 2 hours away to become the administrator of a Christian school. After a couple of months in our new location, John suffered a major brain trauma and passed away within a few weeks. And I mentioned that a few weeks later while I was on a spiritual retreat with the Lord, He asked me to let go of the responsibility I had carried for so many years of caring for my husband, along with the pain and helplessness I had felt at watching my loved one suffer. The Lord asked me to walk back into life.

During the previous 8 years after John's stroke he had extreme limitations, and I had not been able to be involved in ministries in the church. I could barely go for an hour on Sundays, and only with one eye on my phone in case I were needed at home. The Lord had been extremely faithful to give me strength, love, and compassion day after day. I was grateful I was able to take care of my husband through it all. But I must admit there were times when I missed being a real part of a church family during those years.

When the Lord had asked us to move, I had looked at the areas around the school. The school was set in a rural location, with a city to the north up over the hills, and a larger city to the south. I started looking for housing in the southern city. I have family members who lived in the city to the north who urged me to consider living there, since I would be closer to them, and real estate there was not as expensive. I looked it over and even took a test drive one day while visiting the area. It seemed a reasonable alternative to seriously consider living north of the school. Just before going to sleep that night, I prayed about it, seeking the Lord's guidance. Early in the morning the Lord approached me with authority. He told me emphatically that He wanted me to locate in the city south of the school. Since this whole move was being accomplished in obedience to every detail of God's leading, I wasn't about to disregard His direction. I was grateful that He had been so strong and clear in His guidance.

I started looking for houses in the southern city and began to consider churches in that area. This was the time of COVID, so most churches were streaming their messages. It quickly became apparent to me which church the Lord was leading me to. On the next trip up to the area, I was going to meet with the current school administrator to talk about the details of God's plan for me to work at the school. Before I met with her, I went by the church I had found and sat in the courtyard there and prayed for them. I prayed for their new pastor, his family, the church members, and their fellowship. After we moved to the area, I started attending for an hour on Sunday mornings, when I could make it while taking care of John.

After John had gone to be with the Lord, the Lord made it clear I was to be more active in life, which included church life. I gladly started going to the church's prayer groups. Then I got involved in music ministry and a small group. It was such a joy to be able to fellowship with these encouraging believers. They were welcoming and friendly. Very quickly I was rejoicing in being part of a church family again. One of the men in the prayer groups, Jerry, asked me how he could pray for me. He knew that I was the new administrator at the school, and especially with COVID making things difficult, there were plenty of prayer requests over the next few months. As it turns out, Jerry had lost his wife 2 years before. He had loved and cared for her during her illness for a number of years before she went to be with the Lord. We started having some deep conversations about things we hadn't been able to share with anyone else. We understood what we had walked through with our loved ones and were grateful the Lord had given us His help and strength.

What began as a prayer filled friendship, quickly developed into something deeper. When I realized that I was falling in love with this man, I was in shock. I thought that I would be living the rest of my life as a widow. Even though John had made me promise to consider loving someone again after he was gone, I could not fathom the work it would take to develop a new and close relationship with someone else after all these years. I also didn't want to try to start a relationship based on filling a void or a need in my life. I was determined to turn to the Lord to meet my needs. I wondered if I would ever again be able to love someone sacrificially, after doing so for over 25 years. It wouldn't be fair to love another man with less than 100% commitment, with a willingness to meet their needs and consider their desires. I would only want to love someone for themselves, not for what they could give me. I couldn't even begin to wrap my mind around how to develop intimacy again with anyone else, so I was not looking for someone at all. When I realized the depth of the relationship that was developing, I had to run (not walk) to the Lord and pour it out before Him. I did so more than once, especially since I knew this would also affect my family who were grieving the recent passing of their father. The Lord had helped me walk through the grieving process for over 2 years, but their loss and grief was still very fresh for them. But it was undeniable that the Lord had brought someone exceedingly special into my life. Jerry was saying that he loved me and wanted to take care of me. This wonderful man said the Lord was putting it on his heart. The Lord reassured me several times that this relationship was from Him. I marveled at the depth of what was happening so quickly. God told me that this was His plan and was a gift from Him.

Since Jerry and I liked exploring, we were planning to go on a hike through the redwoods early one morning. That morning before I got out of bed, I was talking to the Lord. This new relationship which was filled with such loving care was overwhelming to me. The Lord had shared with me several times in the previous year that since I had believed and obeyed Him, He was going to bless me. When He had said it, I sank to my knees marveling that my wonderful Lord purposed to give me a blessing. I praised His name and thanked Him for His love. I thought that the blessing would mean a closer walk with Him. Now the Lord reminded me of His promise to bless me. He said this relationship with Jerry was the blessing that He had in store. And He reminded me of His authoritative command to locate in the city to the south. If I had not done that, I would not have attended this church or met Jerry.

I was astounded at the amazing details which the Lord had orchestrated in order to bring Jerry and I together. We were both very similar in many ways. One of the best things about our relationship was our desire to love and obey the Lord with all our hearts. Our times together always started with prayer. We were trying to honor the Lord in all that we did. What an incredible thing the Lord was doing! I was humbled by it and very emotional. The Lord asked me that morning around 4 a.m. to accept what He was doing. Little did I know the surprise that was in store that morning.

We arrived at the edge of the redwood forest just before 8 am. We started hiking around a hill that led upward through the shadowed hall of the giant redwoods. Green ferns extended their fronds into the air as they clung to the side of the hill we were climbing. When the trail leveled out, we entered a beautiful, majestic grove of redwoods. The deep quiet reinforced my sense of wonder and reverence as I stood in this temple made without human hands. The redwoods always reminded me of the majesty of God and made me want to sing His praises.

In awe I gazed upward on every side as Jerry led the way to a carved redwood bench where we could sit down. The beauty around us was breathtaking. As I sat down on the bench, I turned and realized Jerry was kneeling. I thought that maybe he was going to pray for our outing that day. I was totally clueless until Jerry started telling me how much he loved me, how special I was to him, and then he asked me to marry him! I was stunned, you could have knocked me over with a feather! I uttered his name in shock and surprise. Then I realized why the Lord had taken such care to talk to me that morning about the blessing He was giving to me. He wanted me to accept Jerry's marriage proposal. I knew Jerry enough to know that he was giving me his whole heart and pledging his love to me for the rest of his life. I was able to freely respond with great love and gladness by saying, "A thousand times, yes!"

After a few months of courtship, we were married in front of our church family right after the morning service, giving testimony to the amazing love and work that God had done in our lives. Our mourning had been turned into joy. We will never forget or stop loving the spouses we were married to for so long. They taught us so much about what a loving marriage relationship should be.

And we rejoice in what God is doing now. His love is so incredibly beautiful and full. As we follow Him and love Him with all our hearts, He makes our love beautiful and full and more marvelous than we could have possibly ever dreamed. I realize now that all of the difficulties which had kept me from seeking a new relationship were wiped away with the simple act of loving someone. It is not difficult to have intimacy, to share everything, to give sacrificially when you love someone. Love fills the heart with great joy. And it is not difficult to surrender and trust the Lord with all that we have and all that we are when we love Him. May the Lord continue to teach us how to love each other deeply, to love Him completely, and to invest our lives in following Him wherever He leads.

ACKNOWLEDGEMENTS

This has been a most unusual writing experience. After being remarried for barely one month, the Lord let me know that it was time to start writing this book. He gave me chapter headings and directed when it was time to write. Sometimes the chapter headings were daunting, yet the focus of the writing became clear each time. I was to share what God had shown me in my walk with Him. He is great and glorious. Much like the facets of an exquisite jewel, it takes all of us to reflect back even part of who He is and what He can do through our lives. To Him goes all the honor and the glory; His love is everlasting.

My dear husband was incredibly patient, understanding and encouraging of this whole process. While I wrote, Jerry prayed. As one of my editors, he offered unfailing inspiration and honesty and urged me to press on. He is such an unexpected blessing from the Lord for which I will always be eternally grateful.

My children have walked this journey with me. They are such examples of courage and love. They supported and cared for their Dad in so many ways. I am grateful I have the privilege of being their Mom.

I received such tremendous encouragement from my dear sister in Christ, Damia Dillard. She knew the details of what the Lord shared with me over the last few years. I worked with her in healthcare, and I know her heart which overflows with deep compassion.

I deeply appreciate the support provided by my pastor, Marttell Sanchez. He continues to speak the Word of God with grace and unwavering dedication to the truth.